Hannah Augusta Kimball

Socio-Economic Mythes and Mythe-Makers

Hannah Augusta Kimball
Socio-Economic Mythes and Mythe-Makers
ISBN/EAN: 9783337180249

Printed in Europe, USA, Canada, Australia, Japan
Cover: Foto ©Suzi / pixelio.de

More available books at **www.hansebooks.com**

Socio-Economic Mythes

AND

Mythe-Makers

BY

YOURS TRULY

BOSTON
ARENA PUBLISHING COMPANY
COPLEY SQUARE
1896

Copyrighted, 1896,
BY
ARENA PUBLISHING COMPANY.

All Rights Reserved.

ARENA PRESS.

Socio-Economic Mythes

and

Mythe-Makers.

To mould the general thought, to direct the social aim, within the breast of man to waken mother-feeling; dear reader, may this be yours and mine.

Reverentially Dedicated
TO THE
Cause of the Gods of Society.

Of vicious class legislation we have overmuch. But more, give us more of equality's pure white wine. Into the Golden Goblet pour, pour. Stop not. Equality-legislation ne'er can overflow. Each shall quaff, and ALL shall be happy.

CONTENTS.

CHAPTER.		PAGE.
I.	Mythes and Mythe-Makers,	7
II.	Mythes and Mythe-Makers (Cont.),	44
III.	Society's Movements Outlined,	77
IV.	Socio-Economic Facts,	96
V.	Confusion of Socio-Economic Facts. Political Economy an Imaginary Calculus,	107
VI.	Confusion of Socio-Econonic Facts. Political Economy an Imaginary Calculus (Continued),	138
VII.	Social Law the Economic Law,	201

SOCIO-ECONOMIC MYTHES AND MYTHE-MAKERS.

CHAPTER I.

MYTHES AND MYTHE-MAKERS.

THE growth of the race soul, like the growth of the individual soul, keeps pace with a rational exercise of the reasoning power; therefore that which hinders rational exercise, hinders the unfoldment of the God within us (reason), hinders our moral and spiritual growth; and this is done by imprisoning mind within the sphere of ignorant thought. Minds unconscious of the universality of reasonable relation, do, in their gropings after knowledge, pass through an era of savage thought, the era's length and depth of savagery being in direct ratio to poverty in perception of reasonable relation's certain law. Etymological authority defines mythes to be fabulous or imaginary statements conveying an important truth, the mythes themselves implying a claim to supernatural power ; respect for actual facts should have led to the substitution of the term *concealing* for the word *conveying*.

Mankind, by reason of its birth into a larger field of conscious reasoning, is ever seeking the "why" of its environment, and though the field in which we query be much expanded, yet the tendency to question is not limited ; for the inquiring disposition is in essence just the same, be it exercised by savage or by sage. And this propensity, is it not one of twin essential factors in all progress, being an internal motor, speeding race and individual along the evolutionary highway of planetary life ?

It is to be expected that mythes will follow in the trail of phenomena, as they are the outcome of mutually acting modes of existences ; mind, and things outside of mind, compelling its attention. Love of the marvellous, joined to blind conservatism which clings alike to truth and error, does, in an era of looking *at*, not looking *into*, things, naturally breed mythes, therefore whole regiments of chaotic theories invade fields which rational explanation, given the chance, clears of knotty stumps; and mythic stumps, are they not, on the fair land of intelligent reasoning, unsightly excrescences like Pinkertonism, that blot upon our Republic's national existence?

Accepted as sound interpretations of the real, mythes are to knowledge formidable barriers, acting like a hedge across a highway to a footsore traveller, leaving him no alternative but waste of energy, climbing over contrivance useless, wicked, or cessation of his further onward movement. Mythes live and fatten by the credence given by acceptance of them as final, as real truths. Consequently, along all lines of travel barricaded by these illusionary giants intellectual progress is repressed, and, by preventing social conduct from becoming human, we are robbed of an earthly heaven, and the soul's growth is stunted by an utterly unsolvable problem, by a mythe. For how can men, with natures which unfit them for the art of making heaven here, be admitted into one in the hereafter, and there in heavenly soil take immediate root? The thing is unnatural; the very thought is unthinkable.

Nowhere throughout the kingdom of relation does the principle of heredity unimpeached hold sovereign sway, save in the fact that savage action has its birth in savage thought, and both stand outside the domain of human morality.

Twofold is our source of knowledge: experience of things *outside* of self, experience of things *within* the self; but their value as intelligence depends upon the amount of *rational* discrimination used.

Mythes are vapors escaped from misty mental space. To deform the language is baby's prerogative, else how can it utter infant thoughts? Expression cannot rise above the level of its intellectual power; no one questions baby's right.

Equally unquestionable is the natural right of savages to build and hold unto their mythes. Only the fool expects that for which neither power nor opportunity exists, but only the fool rests content with shortage, when for the greater "which" both power and opportunity exist. It is he of weak sight who turns from the brilliancy of electric illumination, preferring the help of feeble candlelight. The sun wakens to busy life its Eastern peoples, the while tarrying in its call to Western folk. Were it possible for an accountant to procure at a given hour the results of the toil of mortals, could true judgment be passed without taking into account the fact that sunlight comes to different parts of the earth at different hours? Is it then unreasonable to expect some extra legitimate claim upon the advanced races and of them some special expectation, in the calculations of evolutionary time?

Therefore, when science and scientific art, the intellectual weather-vanes, point to a longer stretch of race life, indicate a sooner sunrise in evolutionary time, and yet there is found among such people mythe-making, polished and refined, serving as a lucrative class trade, with such anachronism, I ask, what can a body do but denounce it as——? As the ocean is to a drop of its watery contents, so is the present unfoldment of industrial power contrasted with the early days of economic production; and yet, simultaneous with improvements in industrial methods, simultaneous with easy production, goes a lessening of chance to *enjoy* the comforts produced; and the laboring class — upon whom society depends for its existence, upon whom social jugglery fixes the doing of real work — finds its individual members in a state of continually increasing economic insecurity through the geometric increase of their spoliation.

Not a few savants, politico-economic (real sharpshooters they), aim at the solution of this socio-industrial problem, but, missing the mark, their powder soils the skies, while over the social gladiatorial ring this social (?) fact in herculean might is master still, is unhit by their senseless verbiage. From the kingdom of being why learn we not a lesson? Among inferior animals, the individual members as well as the species go the length of their spiritual tether. The very *trees* obey a natural law of growth, while superior animals act as if privileged to interfere with natural principles and laws of dealing with each other. True modes of settling what is right, modes natural to *real* humans, are disregarded; and so is trampled upon, and trampled out, the individual's and the species' opportunity to *rapid* increase in intellectual, in moral perception. Borne in space upon the bosom of his mother earth, each mortal has freedom to life-giving air.

To the intelligent social observer, the biological as well as the physical fact of position demonstrates the divine dictum — equal natural right of each individual with every other to grow, to unfold, and to adjust itself in the spacial conditions of that race's social environment into which such individual is born; the adjustment to be not by artificial means (money's vile decree), but through laws of God, laws of natural adaptation. And why should not the force beckoning each to his, to her, socio-economic position, fixing size and extent of its space, be a natural attraction, a law of atomic social gravitation, which is nothing more nor less than the capacity to enjoy, the ability, the willingness, to do some socially useful thing.

Behold the celestial world, where through the universal and impartial operation of great nature's law, each atom in space seeks and finds its right abiding place; so might each *human* atom, by the natural inherent force of its own soul's evolution, unerringly find *its* true spot in social space but for—— Now, were society unarrested in its possible onward motion, were its speed not broken, its wheels not clogged, then would all, then would each, go forward rapidly on evolution's progressive track, a moving equilibrium like the solar system, which grandly pierces space; a unified, diversified whole. To the cheek of every honest social thinker, if intelligent, is brought the blush of shame when beholding the unhuman exhibit of division into classes, those who produce, and those who pillage, albeit by "legal" means. Nevertheless this social solecism, bastard of human intelligence, this rape upon divine law (the mathematic test of right to possession), engages in its defensive warfare the *intellectual* efforts and the useful fortifications of economic mythe-making.

Accepting in the main Herbert Spencer's statement, that there is a soul of truth in things erroneous, I am yet constrained to say that, in the case of economic mythes, this soul is so attenuated that its truth reaches us in about the same period of time it takes light to travel to the earth from the farthermost conceivable fixed star. Mythe-makers are they who account for the existence and order of things in a fanciful manner. As the zoölogist builds up intelligence by unwinding the thread of biological continuity, tracing the relation in time of existing species to their progenitors of the dim and misty past, so likewise the social paleontologist, by light of evolutionary truths, is able logically and historically to trace through past variations and modifications our present mythe-making species to its primal protoplasmic form.

Turning from the phantasies of an occasional writer, which leave small doubt that in his judgment our race was at creation poised on topmost peak of intellect's high cliff, we find that psychological as well as historical facts warrant the belief in a savage period for our race. Literary dissection, if conducted in obedience to legitimate principles of search and research, strips the object in hand of its deluding appearances, standing it forth clothed only in the garb of naked truth. Of the modes of demonstration, I leave to a later chapter the practical verification, by direct investigation of the mythes themselves. If a general view be an intelligent and logical presentation of the subject-matter, to the reflecting mind is brought home a few cogent conclusions, and it is perceived that like causes produce like effects; that differences in method and differences in degree constitute no difference in kind.

At society's dawn it is probable that individuals were on a par in the then rude art of mythe-making. The principle of differentiation was and is ever moving; none disputes its noiseless, certain tread, albeit much distorted in its travel, being hampered in its individualizing work. Still, in spite of epileptic seizures, on it goes in helpful company. Principle of heredity, hers no mean jog-trot; surely she has the right of way to do, when *demanded* of her, a most heinous work. In the lower zoölogical kind, social instincts (divine marvel) did seed and bud, but in human folk they blossomed out. Human language, subtle, meaningful symbol, may be used to hem ideas in; therefore it is likely that ability to manipulate the language was no small factor in the social differentiation in the creation of the mythe-making class; but for their perpetuation, heredity and other potent causes have sufficed.

In early times, as now, desire to excel made the explanations of the more fanciful few beyond the comprehension of themselves and others, consequently acceptable to all. So much for their origin. But in causes of perpetuation we have on hand a something manifold in nature, causes inside, causes outside; and many-shaped is this conglomeration of matter. We can trace a large share to a sense of subordination which comes from mistaking the astral of superiority for superiority's real self. Trifling is the blunder, yet it makes us wade in the wake after phantasie's delusive sail. The curb-bit in the mouth, the bridle on the head, we know the feeblest rider may retain control of a noble steed; but let that horse once feel his own self-power, what is the situation? Rider sprawling. So long befooled, the many have become mentally inert, seem not to realize that they can look behind, on either side, ahead; are hindered; wearing old blinders yet, have come to think them their actual flesh and bone.

In the affair of mythe-perpetuation there are fine ingredients, among them self-conceit, sometimes taking form like this: What I or mine have held must indeed be right; to instance which I quote responses to an oft-put query: "Why are you a Republican or why a Democrat?" "Well, really now, I don't quite know; can't think of any reason for my party principles, my political belief, except it be — well, you see, my father, he was one." There is a reason for mythe-perpetuation which is most unworthy. It arises from mismating our consciousness of the relation between wrong deeds and intellectual mistakes, with creation-creed. From this wedded, disunited pair, come forth queer notions as to the whence and the where should fall future suffering. Mistakes, want of knowing, breed suffering. This the dullest feels and therefore knows. Maybe he has experienced disappointment, having taken to a May-day picnic a wrong direction. Ah! did he but note that suffering ceased when the error in direction was corrected by *himself*.

In order to make plain the reason to which I here allude, I must emphasize the feeling, our consciousness of the mortal source of suffering; for this certitude, coupled to our misbeliefs, induces the great majority to continue letting others think for them. The intellect not doing rightly its rightful work, its uncleared vision sets the limit of the individual's, as of the social horizon. If with chains one should load the feet, could they move? Neither can the shackled intellect. Sensed is the relation between cause and effect. Upon the existence of suffering we agree. The "divide" is: who is to bear it, you or I? Ignoble followers of a lead hold it should be, not those who *receive* intellectual errors, but those who *give* them. Too confused to keep distinct and separate in our thought that which is divine from that which is simply legal, we, the great majority, think them synonyms, and act accordingly, believing that not for *us* is heaven's avenging decree; for have we not been obedient? have we not shut our eyes? The sun is a fickle monster, is not steady in welldoing, acts erratically, of his smiles we are not certain, turns his back on earth, leaves us freezing; then, too, by his fiery flames we are scorched. From the inconstant way in which the sun does act, I conclude it is "obsessed"; there is a man in it.

Tracing wrongs and disasters to Father Sol, we, the great majority, by savage metaphysics swayed, connect woes yet to be attained with an edict from the skies. But to help themselves out of prospective mire the believers deem it natural that future punishment should fall upon the heads of those who intellectual errors breed ; and I have a secret to declare which shows matters down fine : by their flocks shepherds are consigned to an avenging deity who, it is assumed, is now lying in wait with divine intent, vengeance.

Now, were we *real* believers in that process (evolution) which we see, we should know that in the domain of natural decree there is no room for mythes. One may suffer *with* but never *for* another.

We should further know, that each one having powers makes progress only by their unfoldment. Let us hearken to the cry of reason; set her free. She will work a brilliant, bloodless revolution by great discoveries from the plainest, simplest facts. One boy gives unto another apples, sour, unripe ; is there room for query to which falls the suffering gratuity, which enjoys the stomach-ache, him that gives, or him that takes? Wherefore is there breach between us and the Father-Mother God ? Can it be, I wonder, that the ditch is digged by them that are in it ?

And now I think upon it, how strange that those nearest to Supreme Wisdom deal in intellectual rubbish ? Oh pshaw ! after all, I guess that the institution of legalized "preach" is not divine, but simply human. Pious Fathers of the near past, prompted by a mythe of individual right divine to do the work of fiend (when backed by church and state), did perpetrate hideous social blunders, tied to faggot and to stake wicked dissenting brothers. These God-loving Fathers knew right well that, faggots lighted, neither prayers nor imprecations availed to stay consumption of their helpless prisoner. Pious Fathers had "knowledge" of relations. All manifestations may in classification be simplified down to things and to relations. Things by the senses are perceived, but relations by effects are felt; pleasantly when human, painfully when there is sinful misplacement. Fire is not man's natural element ; to be in it is to sin, is to suffer. Facts stand firm. Continual experience demonstrates that all sins are forgiven save one. "Sin against the Holy Ghost," sin against right relations, is not, cannot be, forgiven while persisted in.

Prompted by the jural instinct, and with the hope that I may something more than amuse, I intend to give of the mythic art instances culled from records curious of our race's early past, of those days when human deeds differed so from ours, deeds at which you will be shocked. Still we are charitable and just, allowance making for the conduct of those early men, for then the species *all* were savage and *none* were Christianized.

I beg that you'll bear in mind that to obtain the matter I shall present required laborious toil, much archeological work. Now, were I giving a graphical description of later ways of doing, different would have been the character of my effort. For books abound, descriptive, narrative; the literary warehouse is crowded, is overflowing with expositions and with travels; in it a "sensitive" feels uncomfortable, feels attacked by a whole menagerie, untutored, wild.

To picture a social past it is essential to have

a clear perception of contact or relations. This gives to one a view of "probabilities", and the mode of their application to the "say-sos" to determine which of them is true. Thus equipped it is safe to venture, but without these mental stilts one is sure to be "snowed under" by the chaos and confusion in the books. If so prepared, entrance within the literary enclosure is no hazard, being qualified to reconnoitre contradictions, brilliant guesses, mistakes, and even downright lies.

You will be surprised, I wager, to see how many of the statements (big bullies) kill each other; but with these of course you have nothing to do except look calmly on and see the murder; lots of fun it is, too. With others there is work to do, chopping, overhauling, fitting angles; and maybe there's chance for pruning and grafting. With some assertions I have found occasion for tender care, they containing way down deep, quite smothered out of sight, the faintest spark of intellectual light. Still, when they are sometimes something in themselves, because of their interpretation, or because of their false position, the majority of social affirmations are found to be ridiculous, fit only to be flung out of truth's sweet heaven. Yet do not despair, do honest, straightforward work, and you will get something true, therefore something presentable.

To give word-picture of the ways and doings of our ancient past did indeed call for much gleaning; still in that search, if I found less literary *hay*, I also found less literary *stubble*. If facts precipitated by pen or picture do reflect the state of mind, then in early time the people all believed in and practiced necromancy; acted as though they thought the constitution of an act could be altered by simply changing the position and direction of its original initiative motion; as if black, starting from the north or east, could on its line of travel white become; but should the blackness turn and come from south or west, why, then there would be no such marvel.

To help the matter out there were forms and

ceremonies which all allowed could set aside—
not only *one*, but *all* divine decrees. Whether
the rites, having social bent, were performed on
open square or within four walls, the pictures
failed to disclose, but this thing was apparent:
one of their number, master of the ceremonies,
I suppose, appeared to act as judge, and sat, or
rather squat, from the rest apart, on something
like a pedestal; quite gotten up was he, though
not with cap and gown; *his* riggings were mere
toggery.

I'm asked the picture story? Well, truly, to
me it seemed to say, these men had scarcely
been awakened from the sleeping spiritual state
which held them bound when they were akin to
monkeys and engaged in plays arboreal. The
men conducting the proceedings, which, not
knowing their true nature, I am forced to dub
judicial, appeared to be divided into opposing
sets, and their fierce grimaces gave to the whole
affair a look of strife unholy; a show, if not
gladiatorial in name, at least in nature. When
I have told you all I learned, you will agree with

me that though disjointed is the hieroglyphic form of narrative, yet by a picture's silent speech much is made known.

But before I further go in this direction, I must atone for an omission by giving explanation of the purpose of those judicial (?) proceedings I found pictured; later on I intend to deal with their style and character. If in a fit of passion or for any reason known to savage mind, one man did kill his fellow, then upon this slayer, wretched victim of forces within and forces without, pounced society's *male* thought and action, and, by some means and in some manner, butchered the poor wretch, who, unlike itself, had killed without deliberation, killed without calm reasoning's guidance, killed without acquainting intellect. When adjudged guilty of foul murder, the helpless creature had no hope, stood no kind of show; for how could he, with revengeful brothers bent upon his slaughter, each one in his own soul a murderer of some degree, made so by thoughts black in their character?

And now we have reached a peak, a social act, from which to get good view of intellectual ravines and social chasms. From the practical necromancy of these ancients we infer their belief in the magic art, belief in its power, through forms, to cleanse from bloodstains, provided the heinous act be collective in its registration. That the Lord should have his own, these savages were anxious; therefore, when the murder was of the unsocialized kind, after engaging in certain purifying rites facetiously styled "forms of justice," there would be deliverance of this monstrosity: "our fellow-sinner we find unfit for earth, we find him to be fit for heaven."

I know I'm giving crass absurdities, and I fear you'll think me chaffing; not so, I'm gravely in earnest, and do protest that this horror was all too often perpetrated. But these things by men are done only while they are savages. Those untamed men, ferocious wretches, thought themselves savants, and knew right well the ins and outs of what they were about; out of unskillful hands they boldly took the God-appointed hour of death, took it by sending heavenward a brother. Now this, to say the least, was ill-mannered on the part of society; it was bad breeding to force into the unseen mansion a guest unbidden. Had those low-bred creatures known aught of etiquette, then, prior to such proceedings, they would through reason have consulted the rulers of the divinely ordered home; learned " if it were agreeable" and in conformity with mighty wishes. This done, how different had been their action! Society had found salvation *from*, not *through*, a bloody deed. Incredible that creatures of our species used their brains so little, imagined that by any kind of means or monkeying they could reverse nature's stern decrees of what is right, of what is humanly natural.

In their description of a plant, an edible, I should expect to find the fungus at its root pictured as its luscious fruit.

Connected with their wicked, foolish ways were beliefs, lack of thought, almost funny; their religion decried " mere morality," taught that salvation came through miraculous transformation, the result of a blind acceptance of a creed; but, equal to the occasion, with forethought it was affirmed that, while on earth believers did sojourn, over their blackness mere belief was impiously inactive.

The promised revolution, whiteness of the creed-accepted character, was to come, however, after death. About this miracle they seemed certain, because beyond the range of mortal touch and vision the time and place for its fulfilment were affixed " out of sight." For all alike, acceptance of a particular creed was deemed safe ferriage to heaven. And yet minds were blank, society's great arms were still, when to make the solitary slayer fit on earth to live, skilful motions were most needed. What poverty of thought was theirs! Nowhere found I it recorded of their individual murderer : " I refuse to accept the benefits of society's magic purge." For inconsistencies reason is not at fault ; she is at her post, is no deserter. Had those gross mortals hearkened unto nature's logic, caught deep meanings, felt the law's great edict through the oneness of all motion; had they watched the driftings of the air, the floatings of the vapor, they had known that man, released from gross flesh, etherealized, can come and go with ease, can travel somewhat as he pleases; had known it was reasonable to expect that one badly treated *before* birth, and *after* too, should, through attraction's lawful force impelling, choose to mingle with familiar scenes, choose to haunt unseen his executioner — society, unhuman and bloody.

Upon the style and character of early judicial proceedings, upon customs connected with the office and its function, and upon the manners of the judge and jury as well as him they called prosecuting attorney, let us now proceed to hold our promised conversation.

First, however, before we start the talk, our minds should be refreshed by certain facts. The people were not socially united, were politically divided into groups, and of these it may with truth be said, that in their points of contact, in their corners on each other, of the angles made, not one was "right." Empires, monarchies there were, and a something which the men with their crooked ideas called a republic. A mongrel thing, truly, and so out of sorts with the name it bore that to have pictured it correctly, symbolically, would be as an ugly and deceptive cur.

Sometimes the high officials were elected by the men, who, with ultra-barbarous thought, styled themselved "the people." "La Couvade."* Great method! By it men capture babies, get possessions unnaturally. So well equipped for heroic work, we should scarce expect men to balk at the appropriation of a word, which, though little, yet for one-sex wearing is a full size too big. Sometimes offices were filled by appointment; but after all it mattered not which way the tree was bent, this side or that, for its trunk was girdled. The difference for the people was not in the corruption, nor in the amount, nor yet in the way venality was man-

---

* A mode by which a savage father appropriated the new-born child; after the birth he assumed invalidism, the mother going about as usual. See "Researches into the Early History of Mankind," by E. B. Tylor, p. 288.

aged, but which political party manned society's piratical cruiser.

Under such conditions we agree that justice never once brought forth a living son; invariably miscarried. Nor is this surprising, when in each human (?) breast were striving good and evil, God and the devil; and from the conduct of those men no doubt exists as to the mastery — as to which, in that struggle of spiritual hermaphroditism, was the one to come off victor.

How different now! The law's administration is lawful; and different too are the laws. Equality reigns supreme. No longer penal, the thought is human. The purpose of law administration is both philosophicial and righteous; and of this be assured, the methods are scientifically humane, the object being to discover and to unfold the God within.

How came the change about? By this question I perceive we have in you a stranger; from the Orient, I presume. The causes of our social revolution are no secret, and later on, when compelled, I will tell. Blest are we; no longer competition, the heinous thing, but fraternal socialism, with its humanizing godly creed, evolution. Those benighted folks had an awful belief in supremacy of evil, supremacy of the devil; had in God no humanizing hope. They really thought competition could not be helped, that it was right and to humans natural. At this I'm not surprised, for they were swayed by a creed whose undercurrent made not for the *good* in them, but for the *evil*.

In their books on moral rescue you will find the point I raise made evident, for at all times upon salvation of an individual only were they bent. No carry-all was their deliverance boat; it fulfilled aristocratic notions, was too narrow for a wholesale work, the direction of its sail always being a "him" to be taken from his bad companions. Now, wherefore did the thought not occur to do no bungling surgery, but skillful work, by taking bad companions *too*, thus making a good job complete. The reason for their myopic thought was a belief in which the devil, a philosophic necessity, posed a permanent fixture.

Among their customs I found courts of equity and courts of law separate; equity was specialized, which must be admitted as relevant evidence of stupidity or rascality, or both. Experience teaches us that when the work of courts is application of the "common law," then they are neither more nor less than courts of equity. Unaccustomed to a separation so unnatural, I was much disturbed by this strange one, was overwhelmed, but I rallied quickly and by patient careful search I unearthed and got the reason why; 'twas no Holy Grail I sought.

To make evident the cause for separation I must revert to movements which logically precede statutory law administration. To a few of their number those rude men consigned the basic part of society's general housework. I must not neglect to mention that during my investigation into the political aspect of early nations, not once was trace of a democracy found; and their ideas of a republic are positively amusing, reminding one of a scene at mesmeric show, of a man with a broomstick lovingly thinking it a baby.

I'm quite alive with the thought of what interesting work in practical psychology it would be to explore their mental structure, arrive, if possible, at an intelligent explanation of such self-hypnotization, by locating its objective cause. Aphasia, you know, is traceable to a cerebral lesion. Now, I hope you will not misconstrue my words by thinking that I have mistaken their trouble for a form of that distressing malady. I am aware that their disorder was different in its kind, still I presume you don't deny it has with aphasia a point of contact in their defective intellection, as evinced by the persistent misuse of the word republic. Had their bodies been embalmed, possibly we might have been supplied with material for our scientific purpose; still, from what I know of biology and the home of thought, it is safe to say that under dissection their brains would after all turn out merely cancellated tissue.

In that particular century, the numbering of

which it suits me to forget, that odd political group thought it had the actual baby, but their individual actions towards each other show that republican reality went down not much deeper than the name.

The means of ordainment for the mighty social function, and the mode of differentiation of those basic few? This your inquiry? Now indeed you have struck bottom, and I beg you will a word of warning take, unless you wish to mire. Waive this question or amend it, lay it on the table. Won't? So persistent? Have it then, a narration of what is unseemly, and on your head falls a retribution.

The means and measures for the ordainment, for the differentiation into the nation's legislators were, to say the least, unmatched, unique; not because of merit, not because of special unction for the work, did they reach the pinnacle of the nation's high estate. Furthermore, "I am permitted to tell" that various varied, queer elements entered into the selection, nomination, and election of the candidates. It was the habit of the chosen few to meet regularly upon a consecrated spot, celebrated for doings not at all times the most moral, and while there engage in a sort of work which figuratively may be called the game of legislative battledoor and shuttlecock. True, themselves allowed it was framing resolutions, passing laws, under conditions orderly, and with manner circumspect.

As I reflect on what I read, and upon the variegated incidents connected with the main events, to my help comes simile's kind aid. Men in squads along a line made up of election points ; in time each squad, by a sort of rotary measure, turned the well-oiled wheel of congressional factory. No accident recorded ; I found these operatives were protected from danger while manufacturing law-products, commodities, which turned out to be the people's opportunities worked up into bags for plutocratic uses.

The logic of events, however, has shown that the work of those skilful operatives was not durable, not lasting, for if the warp was true and good, the filling-in was sure to be rotten raw material, gotten through by help of knockdown argument. In political economy, their great science, I found, in explanation of this instability of legislative product, no mention made of capitalistic caprice, capitalistic will, which was the more surprising, as for all eccentricities of socio-economic production, this was their invariable mode of accounting; therefore about the matter I am still agog.

Their annals said, to one who read between the lines, that during legislative labor strenuous efforts were made to work stealthily and to make no noise. Kindly that intention was, benevolent and modest too; wished not to annoy outsiders, sought not to attract attention. But the time of great noise came, the bursting of these bags.

It occurred in this wise. The packing had been skillful, crowding in and in; machinery was used — banking. Congestion is a dangerous thing; means too much of the circulating fluid in one place; means superflous flesh with an enfeebled heart action. To the individual the result is apoplexy and a journey to the skies. *Society* came out of *its* attack; hers was no individual concern. The pathology was different too; the place of her vitality was not at all congested; its condition, the reverse of that, was anemic. Within the social body matters had solidified, interfering with its healthful circulation, with its hearty action. Life, for the useful organs, was made one continuous, needless struggle by conditions foreign to the social working powers. *Conditions* had to die; and but for barbarity interfering with what was natural by maintaining fossiliferous social structures that should have been cremated long before, *individuals* had no *need* to. Society is living; hers no resurrection, nor yet a reincarnation affair, but a veritable new birth was fraternal socialism.

To return in thought to days of social competition. Of them I barely wish to note an uprising like bubbles on the surface of water in commotion. The people sensed their true relation, called these social geysers "Law and (no) Order Societies." Dirty, tyrannous, their doings.

Do you doubt that there was ample and sufficient cause for equity's distinguishment? Was it not honored in the breach, in its separation from courts administering the statutory laws?

In our discursive journey we have reached a junction point, another stage, into which, thanks to invention's aid, we slip without alighting, and proceed to render polite attention to matters connected with the law administration of those early folks. The jury system was their boast; they said that "matters by it got way down, even to the people." Doubtless, when new, this statement of the institution's powers and possibilities was entirely true, but in the era whose doings I am recounting, it had become, through abuse and trickery, simply the toy ideal of an imagined democracy.

At that time the jury was composed of men only. You say truly such monopoly in social matters was wilful violation of division's true principle, division's guiding rule; but anon, in the requirement made, you will discover adequate reason for male appropriation of the office and the functions of a juryman. For in connection with the selection there was this phenomenal demand: no ideas on the subject-matter held in hand for their solution. With these terms each candidate was expected to comply without skulking, was expected to bring absolute vacuity. Now, *women have ideas*. In the act of their special creation, that "rib"* was not anesthetized, but underwent such transformation that with the essentials of a jury examination women could not contend. Unto men, however, nature had been kinder; to high demands they were fully equal; therefore came it naturally about that they alone "filled the bill."

That exclusive privileges are unnatural, by intuition is at once perceived, by reason is dis-

---

* So possessed are our men with the idea that to take advantage of each other is wise, that Omnipotence, Omniscience, God, is by them represented as first causing Adam to sleep (this avoided resistance to the invasion of natural rights) and then appropriating an organic part of the Adamic property; God doing . . . . that good may come thereby.

cerned ; but, being womanly, intuition was in bad repute ; those men had no use for intuition, and upon reason made small requisition. If in the course of rigid examination for the jury office, the selected betrayed a thought, were that thought as hazy as the milky way, it was all-sufficient to secure him a peremptory rejection ; the examiners surmising, feeling certain, that beneath it, in disguise, lurked a woman.

From tiny anthill to towering mountain, from gentle rivulet's little ripple to angry ocean's mighty dashing wave, things great and small have their causes outside as well as inside themselves. Knowing this, in thought have I wrestled, have inductive effort made, to discover not alone the character, but substance, underlying that phenomenal demand. Do you wish to see how in scientific analysis I succeed, each step testing ? I'm working for no prize, nor with thought of any kind of corner ; my sole reward lies in satisfaction.

CHAPTER II.

MYTHES AND MYTHE-MAKERS
(Continued).

CONTINUING the subject, I now invite the public to come and weigh results of my most careful labor, which it will find in the explanation given of that no-idea requisition made by men upon men in centuries past and gone. The law-hewers (so called), at the time of which we are speaking, ignorant of simple anatomical, simple psychological facts, unvisited by thoughts of unity, thoughts of right relation, to the truths of evolution being strangers, formed their judgments from the *outside* of things ; therefore from their minds was projected this pure creation. Some craniums were empty reservoirs ; such made able jurymen. Easily the anomaly was explained,—special creation, miracle for judicial delectation. On this hypothesis (sound foundation) secure they builded, by arguing in this wise: it must be so, else no room within the cranium for us to pour in wisdom, knowledge. Are you not overflowing with admiration for their sagacity, their power, displayed in bending stubborn facts, realities, to fit judicial needs?

Here in this connection many things are pressing for attention, to one of which, bygone courtly manners, it is time to pay respectful homage. Were I gifted with lawyer-like resources I might promise you amusement, but I'm only a plain body, with intellectual powers just equal to a wrestle with matter of fact in its simplicity; accordingly your entertainment will lack in variety the richness of a pantomime. To be frank with you, my intention is simply an attack upon the mind, requiring no side show, no device to call the laughing muscles into active play. In presenting an explanation, this intention leads me to draw inferences that are natural, warranted by the actual condition of things.

Given, their assumption that empty skulls make able jurymen; given, too, this fact, that certain truths are by us intuitively perceived, in this connection we find ample cause for the uncouth deportment, the abominable clownish manners displayed, especially by him they called prosecuting attorney ; behavior that transformed their halls of justice into something akin to a zoölogical cage. Those judicial toilers realized that to do effective work strong impressions must be made upon the men legally installed as listeners. In the query, how to do it, how to make impressive stamp on what they had sworn in as actual vacancy, they were at sea.

Timely aid, however, came in instinct's helpful promptings. True, they argued somewhat in the fashion adopted by us regulars of the medical profession, when administering one of our "shotgun" multiplicity prescriptions, for they allowed that, of a big noise, a show, some of it must, through ears, through eyes, get in ; some of it must somewhere stick ; therefore, can one count it strange that they figured in contortions, and made hideous grimaces wonderful to see? I think not. But with reverence bow your heads while I whisper this to you : the case was one of *voluntary* martyrdom. Their heroic sacrifice of the human way of acting had for its end and aim the cause of justice; it was to advance the claims of right. Well-meaning misguided folk, their good intentions naught availed, but their generalship did mischievous work. Madame Justice by it was made sick, was, in fact, disfigured. Extant pictures, kept as curiosities in our judicial museums, show that ever after, her nervous system being shattered, she went, during the judicial orgies, protected, went blindfolded, which reveals to whomsoever wills to dig, a mine rich in rare kind of ore : truth.

Another factor in the cause of that no-idea-qualification demand was a desire, indeed to be exact one should say a *necessity*, for matching a pre-existing stupidity, that of the judge. A fine appreciation of high art existed, therefore the people felt that a match between judicial intellects, a match of judge and jury, should not be a failure, but one marriage true.

This I take to be the real reason for examinations so severe, for the watchful rigid care, lest by stealth a woman took the jury chair, and, by this mischance, within their hollow oaks ideas began to sprout.

In their official decrees it was not the custom of those judges to expose domestic goods. Though having in existing facts abundant material on which to base decisions, they yet preferred to import their judicial wares from the grave; and thinking that whatever was is right, they travelled backward over social hill and dale to find a something that had long been buried and was petrified or rotting. Undaunted, the sacrilegious wretches an untimely resurrection wrought, a brand new air giving to their grave affair by christening it "judicial precedent." Such transaction meant nothing less, if nothing more, than a union between a living case and a dead moral proceeding. Being tied by judicial fancy, one may be sure the nuptial knot was not "gordian." To him who is unguided by reason all things are possible, therefore grandfather *may* be made to don his baby clothes. Ah! but wasn't it befitting for those judges to wear headgear, and by it drape the home of courtly sagacity.

Detecting in their use of "precedent" the real purpose—to save from thinking—then was disclosed to my perception the meaning of that squat position in the picture to which I have referred, and I serenely thought, surely an artistic nature may feel actual, even innocent pleasure in something, though it be akin to the hideous, if that something makes apparent the law of symmetrical relationship between the state of body and the creature's state of mind. If one of the legal fraternity during resuscitation of the mummy should plead for disinfectant, protesting that he discovered a disagreeable odor, forthwith he was dubbed violator of their ethical code, and without further parley was ejected from their order as an anarchistic disturber of their healthy peace. Things are changed; when women accepted the judicial chair, among the rubbish cleared out went the pestiferous judicial precedent.

Babies holding fast to nurses' fingers make attempts to walk. To perform the walking feat they need help. Babies are most wise. The male mind, being fanciful, requires ? ? ? ? ? Being orthodox, it believed in the resurrection of the carnal. With keen perception, woman knows that, in the backward travel, dead-idea-"snatchers" have no real stopping place until logical surmising reaches the earliest evidence in time of an expressed social relation. Our women judges look not behind; they know that the beckoning hand of progress is before. The construction of the joints causes the body's movement to be forward, and the eyes are placed in front to aid progressive motion.

Looking backward has its place; not to narrow down ideas, not to shrink up deeds. From its perspective view we may a lesson take, may know the fact of self-existent powers, internal possibilities. This knowledge ours, from its possession flows expansion in ideas and decrees.

Our women judges look before. The mother-thought sweeps the entire social circle, stops at the horizon. Women judges have no need to hunt up faded patterns, can construct their own decisions; but then women take tuition from within, women use their reason.

Indeed you are a little "tot" to ask such big questions as, what is intuition? what is reason? You say that you are. . Quite old enough, I am sure, to digest some portions of mystery's facts. No harm to my little listener shall come from the insoluble character of the mental food I offer her. Well then, little woman in search of knowledge, we must first make ourselves sure of certain general truths. This gives to the understanding a firm footing. Will you deem it all unnecessary if I call attention to the fact that in space there is just yourself and things outside of you? Shortly, in a general way, we shall see that this environment consists of objects and of relations.

Standing out upon the lawn, raising eyes, we look as far as we can ; still not great the visual travel ; soon shut off is sight by the kissing of the earth and sky — by the horizon. Physics tells us why. When at Washington last spring, do you recollect that I called your attention to the difference between our range of sight from the dome of the capitol and the top of Washington monument? When older grown, and you have gone abroad, from Eiffel tower the visual distance will be great compared with these. The difference in extent of vision, and in amount of things perceived, you find, depends upon the height of the pinnacle reached. From this Romola can learn a lesson if she choose; but at present I wish to impress upon her mind the fact, that, although existences are divided into the seen and the unseen, yet when diligently pursued, much of the latter yields itself up to sight.

Did this little girl grow eagle wings, many things now veiled by distance might by her bright eyes be seen ; but she must not forget that behind and within all things that may be known are hidden the Powers. By doings only does the absolute reveal itself; all attempts to strip it of natural clothing are a waste of time and energy, for it is no "nude"; but yet to personify the absolute is the work of savage philosophy. Now, my little delver, true daughter of inductive, of scientific Mother Eve, acquaint me, please, with your ideas as to the meaning of the knowledge-fact. In truth I am surprised; your sense of it gives forth no uncertain glimmer; but let us deeper go, and to your present state of knowledge something add.

Were this chair and table taken from the room, the part of your mind by them occupied would not, because of the removal, become a blank, for having knowledge of them and their uses, you call them into mind just by thinking how they looked. Knowledge, then, consists of mental pictures.

And now the little sage is asking how knowledge is obtained, how the "love-knot" is tied. Not alone by the spiritual entities, intuition, reason, unseen forms of master workman, perceptive power, is knowledge gained, for nature has the mortal well equipped. There are the senses. And yet, Romola, our knowledge of realities is small. To make profitable this pursuit in which we are engaged, it is essential to have clear ideas on a cardinal point, that of direction, for when perception goes not straight, but on the bias— But never mind, by and by this little girl will find that this is what's the matter with the *practical*. Always present, powerful in its silent workings is *direction*. What is the meaning of the weather-vane?

Nationalism having eliminated money profits from the object of production, seldom is there need to darn; but by this interesting recreation you've learned that weaving threads in and out, crosswise of those placed in length, you have a fabric made. I will build on this experience no cob-house, but a sound comparison, calling perception of things and of relations the warp and woof of knowledge, just reminding you that while the weaving process gives substance, it also gives to mental product the texture of its character; therefore, to know realities one must look for facts in two directions. And now, by way of lesson, try to think of something standing by itself, alone.

To be sure you cannot do it, for now look, your feet are on the floor, the floor is made secure by foundation to the house placed on the ground. The house is safe; your feet, the floor, foundation, earth, and house are *things*, while the connection they bear to one another is a *relation*. To make things plainer, let us take this string of different beads. Don't you see that not a bead stands alone; the string runs through them, holding them together. Still, do not ignore the fact that as a means of illustration we have used this string simply to objectivize that which is unseen: a relation. Though relation is not seen, yet its *consequences* are both *seen* and *felt*.

In order that a future great philosopher may not limitations make in her thought of the extent and location of relation, I now invite this little girl to a visual feast of the starry skies. This evening let us fill our eyes, get perception of the vastness of the universe, and the littleness of the earth. Gazing upward this is what we see: the moon grandly piercing clouds, always coming out from shadows, beautiful and glorious. In fullness steadily she moves, faithful to the earth. There's a woman in the moon, not a man. Of the relation between our earth and the sun you have heard, how our planet moves around that great orb, though not to circumvent; the cause of their motional relation is a true parental connection. The sun gives to the earth light and heat; one great reason why a little one I love both lives and grows.

(Ah! nearer to the Infinite, to the source divine, is the soul of little child.)

You have touched upon a marvel never to be solved by mortal mind; but of this my Romola may be assured, there is a Power, a *social* working principle, that holds the starry space in peace and order. Do not grow impatient; to your question I am coming.

Now, my little Miss, see here; when in haste your food is eaten, does not your stomach aching protest against the rude intrusion? To be sure it does. Equally true is it of the mind, that there is need of proper care in the mode of its ingestion.

Have you forgotten that truce of ours to be constantly on the lookout for lessons to be learned from relations? Were you going to Europe would it be enough to know the pier from which you'd start, enough to know the direction you were going? I think not. That your voyage might be comfortable and profitable, it would be necessary to give heed to your equipment. Using reason, dear child, makes you sensible of the truth I would convey by means of simile. By the senses things external are perceived, but relations are discovered by the mind through the operations of intuition and of reason. Touch this book, now you know of something near; sensational disclosure, you felt it. Look upon yon mountain, and how know you it is there? Seeing is sensation, feeling.

In this search for knowledge I hope you'll not complain if asked to make yourself a martyr to the scientific method of its gain. Oh! with horror would your soul be filled did you know infinitely less than *quarter* of the fiendish things done to the victimized by those whose want of knowledge leads to the use of criminal means. It is sweetmeats that I offer; later on, if ill I beg you not to murmur; be solaced by recollection of the present agreeable sensation — feeling. Listen with me to sweet sounds; the air is in vibration, in harmonious motion; by pleasant feelings we know it.

In great-grandpa's yard stands a stately tree, a grand old oak; around it we have frolicked. Its parts, you know, are roots and trunk, branches and leaves; now, do you really think that the substance of the tree is different in the different parts? You are mistaken; the elements or particles of matter which, entering into, make up the body of its being, are, regardless of position for the several parts, identically the same; the difference so apparent is the handiwork of nature, adept in the art of moulding.

In like manner the *senses* are connected with each other, the sense of touch to the rest playing the part of trunk. We are cabled to from the outside. The difference in the noise of travel is due to difference in the sense port from which intelligence starts. Conjointly arises the distinctive quality of port, variation in the nervous wires and unlikeness in the character of story to be told, unlikeness of substance in the code transmitted, size and shape, or form, the beauty of diversified color. These are tales having no occasion to make emotional noise; but messages which tell of hardness in the nature of a thing, of resistance, reach the understanding only through a clamor. All disclosures made by the family of senses are sensational, the difference in refinement being caused by influence of external environment. On the ocean of the knowable, in our equipment for the voyage, enthroned within are intuition and its lever, reason; they are the intellectual senses, telling of the unseen.

And now your childish face lights up, and calling for the "previous question" your eyes brightly beam. Pitiful the thought, instructors, stultified by memorizing, for ages were unable to perceive the children's mental need, their hunger for real knowledge. A different system now prevails; instruction is educational. *The gods be praised.*

Having seen the function of the senses, we further learn of their reciprocal use as efficient means of testing doubtful messages. If in the judgments of the mind the facts that they portend were admitted as relevant witnesses, then would the philosophic nursery be cleared of "bugaboos" now flourishing in it.

Having your attention, we will proceed to talk first about the difference between intuition and reason, and then later on we will attempt to explain their relation.

In this room hangs the picture of a great philanthropist, Elizabeth Fry. Raise your eyes, and perception of it, like a flash, is immediate. Now, were the portrait in the adjoining room, to perceive it movements of relationship must intervene. Intuition's perceptive work is as the lightning flash, but reason is a cautious mover. By its steady light, which ne'er goes out, but burns with brighter flame, it socializes. Reason discovers truths and facts by means of classification, and harmonizes by getting into line those things which naturally belong together.

Let us suppose, as through the wood you stroll upon a summer morn, from the ground you take a plant, you pluck a flower. The little messenger of light and beauty is, we will think, to you quite new; but if on knowledge bent, and no wise serpent near, pray tell me what would our Romola do? That is quite right as far as it goes. By examination of the plant's essential organs, by the facts of structure and of form (truths of morphology), you would learn where the plant and flower belong, would come to know the little stranger.

But as I'm in want of a verdict, let us "play" that you are a juryman; one of the ideal kind, I mean. Here, Crier, call the Court to order. Now, Miss Foreman, do you twelve, all good and true, agree that the scientific labor necessary to find out a truth is always flashlike, the work of a moment?

Upon the individual person, the mortal self,

the effect of the work of intuition and of reason is to build up emotion's mountain, the spiritual self, which is not done alone by a perception of the relation of things external to one's self, but also by thoughts begotten by recognition of substance, that in itself is simply a relation, and thus to the individual soul is added a finer matter, mother-feeling.

Women have emotions, and the spirit moveth me to say that *they* display the mountain's alpine peak. Great Jove be thanked! Now *men's* emotions, sad to state, are panoramic views mainly of the mountain's baser portion, its grovelling part.

Romola, I beg you'll not be critical with my wanderings in talk; I am stung to it by a recollection of words from stupid tongues.

But now let us seek the relationship of intuition and reason. When upon a wintry morn to school you go, little tracks in the soft white snow are left behind, side by side, two and two. Examined, do they differ? Not a bit. Though found in different positions, yet in size and shape the impressions, in their form, are alike, each pair matching all its mates. Come, tell me why this is so? What, you hesitate? But now reflect, how could the tracks be otherwise than exactly alike, when by identically the same two little feet all were made? Thus it is in the process we call reasoning; every step in it is taken by the understanding, by the soul of reason, for with primal intuition (starting point of individual soul) are impressions taken and disclosures made.

Now, little student, shall we not profit by industrial example, and by dividing the work of teaching have co-operation? I offer a problem to be solved, wondering the while will the answer come from Romola's intuition. Here are a man and woman, farmers; forty acres of land have they worked; nature, rewarding their toil, yielded vegetables, grain, and live-stock. Now, child, unto whom do these things really belong? Reader, it is too good to keep; quick as a flash her answer came: "Why, to the folks who did the work." Well and truly spoken, by unerring intuition.

Romola sensed a right relation, has seen a "Holy Ghost," no glimpse of which was ever caught by political economists, great ones of our late unsocial past. Very nearly did our Romola open her little eyes in a time to have seen the fiery blood-red sunrise of real socialism. Did we but seek tuition only from within, from the higher, the intellectual self, then with hope of success might I bespeak for my grand-niece, as from sphere to sphere on the voyage of life she goes, perpetual harmony, eternal melody. If I bestrode a literary steed, a real Pegasus, I would not seek like Bellerophon to mount unto the skies, leaving behind the work I had but just begun. As the base of a triangle has its sides, and a point from which these lines are drawn, so likewise an effect has its exposition point, where meet, if they be truly taken, the two main lines of an explanation.

To show connection between cause and its effect, can one do better than example take from mechanics' royal realm? There is a fact in physics, and upon it is based weighty matter, speculative and practical, for immersed in a resisting medium, matter, if set in motion, tends, because of inertia, to revert to its original state. The other line of explanation takes its illustration from the kingdom of dynamics, where the vital forces operate. Yourselves the point of application may make.

In zoölogic travel, an amphibian gets homesick on the land, objects to its varied wonders, blinking, shuts out all he can; but to build up mind, things push against him. He longs for repose, for the sameness of the water, where it was easy going with his fins and fishy tail. Nature compromises; while he is a baby, the kind mother lets him, as a tadpole, have his "precedent." To sever arms from body may be an act that is good, or may be fiendish; which, depends upon the working cause behind it.

To kill, has for its inspiration but one kind of motive, therefore, if it be admitted that an act remains the same, it then becomes the business of accounting to explain the antipodal character of esteem in which it is held. Take color; red (if it *be* red) must red *continue*, however much, through cunning art, its *shade* be changed. Hence, to murder has, in moral chemistry, for its initiative, always the self-same elemental impulse—hatred, revenge. Yet folks have thought that, on occasions, the act of murder was providentially provided with a purifying purge—authority. In the late unsocial past, men exercised their muscles, trained their souls, by a wholesale slaughter of each other, and yet in their books is found expressed much horror of that remoter past when men offered up each other as a sacrifice to their devilish God. To moral myopics, by no flight of fancy can consistency of thought be charged. Their ghastly works they called the "Art of War," and vainly thought by that their bloody deeds were endowed with dignity. Murder's hideous face was veiled by forms and ceremonies, social sanction's finery, through a belief that the biggest monster in the gory struggle was rendered a hero, a social saint.

The cause of their wars I illustrate by what,

according to sensation, the thermometer would register—one captain of the social cargo burning up with fever, his rival shaking in an ague chill. Such differences have furnished fuel to light the fires of human battle when nations, Jonah-like, by royal sharks were swallowed up. May not one be pardoned for a sympathetic thought with any kind of monster whose unnatural state should have caused writhings with at least the ——ache? It is all but impossible to account for their un-Jonah-like conduct, huddled in the belly of a shark, and yet so quiet.

I am venturing the remark that it is not surprising if under those circumstances the plutocrats found themselves redundant. The people, I presume, were semi-paralyzed, could not make out how it came about; and no doubt trained scouts were sent from time to time to disclose the mode of its occurence, and by declaring the "special-providence" act, helped the dilemma out. From the abdomen to the head is a tremendous long journey, means a tedious and blood-stained tramp. This it is which keeps the fearful ones back from rising to the throat of *every* kind of shark. The citizens of those rival sharks were filled with wild imaginings, wondering if quinia, given to the royal invalids alike, was an omnipotent specific, and would score a double restorative effect.

Nor was their anxiety unnatural, since, in this illustrative case, death to one meant multiplicity of expirations. Grim forebodings moved the cool-headed and reasonable of the abdominal community (the men) to their usual mode of arbitration, and they fell to fighting. Over the predicament those M. D.'s were in, I'm literally consumed with curiosity. What could have been their management of doses? But for this interesting query I should have here given them the "dead cut;" to notice quack practitioners is so unseemly. It was possible by Cæsarian section to have saved a host of lives by the sacrifice of one. What to do for the hemmed-in creatures must have put those medical professors in a hopeless quandary. Now, wouldn't I like to peer into their mental state. . . . Oh! I have it: thinking those poor folks housed and fed by the monstrous good will of their patient autocrat, they dubbed them paupers, legitimate "material" for inquisitorial experiment by doctors. In trade rivalry those savages found frequent occasions for belligerency, for the Promethean intellect, being bound, was scared by a shadow —"balance of trade."

Were it in my power, had I a camera, some scenes I would picture, but having none, description must continue to suffice. One big country among those nations was politically a psuedo-republic; its inhabitants, a massive conglomeration, styled themselves the American race; and yet not with blankets or with tatooed face were they figured out. It is really true that, by their dispossessors, the real natives were left in sole possession of some few barbarities. To the Dogberry attitude of mind the citizens of that country were in no wise inclined; to write themselves up beautifully was the custom, leaving the saving confessional of sins to deeds. About every atrocity under the sun was in that great country perpetrated by individuals, who were, if backed by money, sometimes sustained by a "tortion" movement of their laws. Could I versify reflection, the refrain would in substance be: had those people but sensed the deep purport of the flag, of the "totem" by them chosen, listened to their silent meanings silently outspoken, then in that great nation each person with eagle vision had seen the rights of every other being to be just as big as were his own ; then from the point of equal doing what is right, that nation's motion as a social star had been true and straight. But, alas! it is with regret I state that the example set by those United States was far less glorious than was needed. Nevertheless, this much can with truth be said : in the treasures of its general thought, equal rights and freedom, a real Pompeii were those United States compared with a socio-political atmosphere laden with the bacteria of feudalism.

Across a river, famous for its sovereign torrent fall, was a little handful of big-feeling folk. My ! but they were savage quite. From blurred letters I barely made out the name "Canuck." Politically it was no pseudo-republic, nor yet was it true monarchy; guess it might with truth be called a hobbledehoy. Now those poor folks paid large sums of money to a man converted into Governor-general by royal pranks. True, they owed him much for arduous and useful toil, his destruction of their pens and ink, his marking with a foreign seal their unlaundried political linen. Situate in "Canuck" was Tarungto, a beautiful city, but wicked and unmoral. One might think in reading of its doings that, mushroom-like, it had sprung from the backwoods, but such surmise is a mistake; it had age, for abundant evidence exists of progressive women living there. If I wished to have the nightmare I would give loose rein to fancy, thinking what must by those liberal women have been endured; quite awful, I am sure, and so I don't care by experience to go further into the matter. The plain truth is, that city was scourged by a plague worse than Job's boils—pious consistency. 'Twas no harm, they argued, to take on the sacred morn milk and cream, provided that at back doors the thing be done ; but to have Sunday street-cars was, to the morally feeble, the piously strong, an offence, a heinous crime. On the road of intelligence belated were those folk, which accounts for weakness of moral vision, obscuring what to the clear-sighted is so plain, that the poor have the right to an opportunity to use Sunday, their only day for an outing, as each chooses, as conscience dictates, and as health requires. With customary regard for accuracy those "remonstrants" to what is right styled themselves Protestants. In solemn conclave met that city's worldly fortunate, and after prayer unanimously agreed that in one's own carriage to ride on the Sabbath was quite the thing, for such an outing smelled not of vulgar sin. But as the sapling conscience demands that something real be done, though just a little will suffice, this is why, to restrain their beasts to a solemn walk or at most a guarded trot was by amendment provided ; and that coachman failing to put on a mask, serious expression, was to be fined.

Of one progressive woman's energetic efforts the records of Tarungto bear trace. Though mammoth the footprints of her social work, yet unlike those of the Eozoön Canadense, they are certain, and of the real human are legible marks. Her sex's pioneer in the medical profession of Canuck, Dr. Emily H. Stowe sought along more lines than one to direct the moral sense, but prejudice and bigotry prevent the wholesome expansion of ideas and of deeds, so about equal rights the well-to-do persisted in caring not a "continental," persisted in flaunting the righteous rag.

Stupid things sometimes show up funny; gossips were those pictures. In a conversation between a gentleman and a lady this amusing incident occurred : An earnest look upon the pictured face and yet he said : "Is it possible, Mrs. Barbalow, you are not aware that in Canuck the people are far more moral than yours?" Her's was a smiling face. I quote verbatim the reply she made, deeming it a "stunner," for it shows how a man's words and acts belie each other: "Do I mistake, or have you not said that having left Canuck for good you have come to the States with us to reside?"

Monsieur, were you asked to name the points of difference between tweedledum and tweedledee, what answer would you make? As I expected, you say that the distinction lies in their orthography. "You lie," vociferates society; "between the tweedle of the dum and the tweedle of the dee behold a chasm deep and wide, dug by us in our high-priest capacity." Indeed, monsieur, it is your turn a question to propose. What's that? Can a leopard change his spots? Yea, verily, I answer. Is the thing not done by Mr. Leopard as in time he learns to shoulder a gun? Humans, having knowledge of constructive art, have repaired a damage that in zoölogic travel they *en route* sustained, but upon that piece of soil, the soul, the tax has been, I own, so heavy as to nearly bring about its reversion to a primal state.

Now, I for one desire to get conclusions

straight, and so in all sincerity this question put: What *is* "male intellect" for anyway, if it be not to make good man's loss of wild-boar tusks and tiger claws? Woman's part in the concern of war is so involved in horror, that I feel to speak of it with bated breath; kindly draw your chair nearer. Taught by men that to breed sons for battle was an heroic service, nay, their pious duty, whose fulfilment was sure by divinity to be rewarded sometime, somewhere, "out of sight," when from battle no portion of the darling boy came home, then to solace the anguished mother was prepared this sweet morsel: to give a bitter lesson the auspicious occasion had by a "Heavenly Father" been improved; her heart's love must from her son be brought home to her God. "For I, the Lord thy God, am a jealous God," men said.

Of woman's relation to divinity I have certitude, I feel that it is proved. Men have "brought her up by hand," have tried, disregarding "the signs," to wean her from the good, but to the mother-thought in God she is moored. An eastern star has risen. In medicine, we descendants of an ancient wizard line, "regulars" in the art of curing patients, shake no sacred rattle; therefore is there hope in all directions for completion of the unfinished business of our prehistoric past. War and murder, individual and social crimes, are estranged, widely different; plain is this to men.

And yet this little girl, Romola, persists in saying that she "don't see it." Over something have I pondered long. Hither come, grandniece, and learn the results of my much cogitation; hear the judgment of my mind. In the mystery of being, individualization has its ultimate objective aim, which to me, no longer occult, seems quite plain. From relevant, from weighty evidence, I conclude that the purpose of earth life, with its bother, is to make a "grant" unto a needy class, is to relieve a poverty. *With human intellect our men must be endowed.*

CHAPTER III.

SOCIETY'S MOVEMENTS OUTLINED.

FRATERNAL socialism is the destiny of society. This conclusion verified by interpretation of its progress, by the light of the facts of motion.

Voyaging through space is our solar system, the sun, planets, and their boon companions; naught interferes with the majesty of their movements, and naught interrupts their onward equal motion.

Society, when its beginning? Where its early morning? We have an exhibition of co-operation among the ants and bees, little folks, beings in the kingdom of invertebrata. A sort of instinctive freak, I do suppose, but yet it shows us, who are evolution's fine productive work, what are *our* social possibilites did we but *use* our intellects. As species multiplied, and diversified forms came on with rapid stride, there was interruption of this co-operation's line of march, consciousness of self becoming the omnipresent, all-powerful feeling; and so association, blest work of power co-operative, of principle social, though not wholly discarded, at least met with the cold shoulder, socialism being "quite too sentimental" for denizens of bigger fleshly homes. Although the pasture is poor, association browses on, ne'er quits the living field; conscious of her guiding spirit, eternal principle, she is scientific, and knows with keen prevision that some day her soul shall have a beautiful complete expression, albeit the process is piecemeal.

In the mammalia her debut was attended with supernal glory, for against the possibility of calamitous mishap the social principle came guarded, protected by maternal emotions, came fixed in mother love. Oh! wise provision. The zoölogical argument prevents the assumption of a completely individualistic period for man, at the same time logical thought bars the supposition that social progress, shown to be evolving, could have been severed in its evolution course by man, the superior animal. Why, the thing is unthinkable, the humanizing principle put out of humans' great primary. Why, those men were not afraid of being "sentimental," therefore for the human species, from their very first, we must postulate the social state, not indeed fraternal, but one disjointed, mangled in its form, filial love for which keeps male intellects upon the rack, busy devising ways and means to retain a burden, a prehistoric mummy. There *is* comfort. Final disappointment awaits all efforts out of time, out of tune; and paternal socialism, dear fetich, is already doomed, soon will find its true abiding place in musty annals of the social past. Fraternal socialism, long overdue (ways most sinister delay the birth), must wait till a social whirlwind, sweeping, rends asunder the barriers. Among the truths demonstrated by philosophical science is the fact of universal motion. Substance, ever changing its position, obeys the continuous call of a tireless taskmaster — "principle of activity." Therefore may we not conclude that as soul and matter are tied up in one, they together ceaselessly are on the equal move?

What is the meaning in the cosmic drama of the part played by direction, meaning of the power to become? On this particular head not much is often or intelligently said, except in scientific art where the importance of direction is made plain ; for in the mechanical realm men recognize that a chance for error breeds disastrous results, so there is patient, careful observation and no trifling with its "how ;" and of course ways and means result from honest analytical work. Therefore it is proven beyond doubt, that, impulsion granted, the direction of a moving body is the resultant of the forces acting on it from without. Furthermore it is shown that cessation of all motion is an affair of appearance only, and that when arrested in its progress a body transfers mass motion to its molecular or individual parts. A weighty body, great momentum, obstructed in its course, friction of the individual particles, ignition, flame, destruction of the mass.

Yourself may make the social application. Journeying upon life's highway are beings, exhibitions of its wonders, and when, to powers attained, new energies are called out from lifepower's mystic space, such display is stars plucked from skies and made one's own. Whence comes it, and what is it that interferes with the race's majesty of movement? What interrupts the equal onward motion of its individual parts? A mass of molecules is society; their movements summarized are motions from point to point in the state of association, particles, combination, masses. To stop here one might truly say that the process on its surface differs not from the formation of a stone.

But while recognizing points of contact through the facts of motion, let us not be hasty in conclusions. There are differences to note. Like and unlike is an omnipresent fact. Were it otherwise, where would be the work for Reason? She would be idle; a heinous thing.

Prior to intelligent discussion *this* must be recognized : in the depths of the sea of knowledge are certain bottom facts, and worthless is that literary image that pictures them afloat. According to position, and order in time, causes must be grouped, classified, otherwise the notice received is not comformable to the force of their active work, and by *that* kind of literary effort just nothing is bespoke. Fruitless is the reasoning when an essential fact, like the principle of true division, is maltreated, cast upon its back. Which of us cannot recall instances of dire confusion when primary causes, those first in time, soonest at the work, met with scant polite attention. It is gleeful, while the learned " are giving higher utility to ink," to watch the vulgar scramble into which first causes are forced with their secondaries, those which are born effects, but, by reason of relation, don the kingly purple and exercise control.

I own it is painful to find internal and external causes, a staid worthy couple, maintaining throughout their sober walk down time the circumspect position, each keeping from the other a respectful distance; painful to find them through queer reasoning's whirl joined in a merry frolic, which, to say the least, is inconsistent with the stately measure of their natural tread. Internal and External Cause, estimable pair, have you a grievance? Are you mismated? True, I do perceive a difference, but is it matter for despair if, within her bosom, *Internal* bears the vital spark? Contented be, External; *thine* the art to *call it forth*, a heavenly flame.

The motion that we predicate of stick or stone has its initiative in the mortal will, takes its first leap from mortal throw; but this assumption for the primal internal cause of social impulse would indeed be vain. Principle of self, smooth down that ruffled plumage; with you I have no quarrel; do I not know that your birth was in immortal will, your leap was by divine throe? Yet, sir, I have a quarrel with the persistent stupidity of your ways of doing social things. Sweet principle of sympathy, latest come to earth from heaven, not yet thy golden head canst rear aloft, not yet in thine own true sphere canst walk erect; there is an enemy in ambuscade — stupidity.

Science declares that were it possible to eliminate all external resistance to onward motion, then a body would continue forever in a straight line moving in the direction given it by original impulse. Now, if this assumption be logical of motions, mortal in their origin, is its application, I ask, less logical, certain, or less true, to motions (beings) having for their initiative the divine, the God impact? Wherefore, then, within a race (the great social body) is there such halting, limping, bobbing up and down, in short, the sin of uselesss, unnatural commotion. In the beginning all were uncivilized; now, explain why our social body, an intellectual mosaic, is not also a social plane; such is the domestic family.

The reason I will try to make plain, for everything has its "why." Causes are within, say you? Agreed, *within* the individual and *within* society. We both are satisfied as to the "where" to look for causes and occasions, primary and secondary; yet I would not have you think me one of those of conditions so peculiar that I hesitate to call them folks (lest it be a misnomer), who, by a process of invagination, have parted company with senses for the external, have become all *inside*, which accounts for irrational idealists denying the working mode of God, subject and object in relation.

And now, before we further talk, grant me this favor: load me not with literary gewgaws, explanations, tinselled jewelry, "glittering generalities;" deal with facts, be explicit, and, in short, "come down to dots;" tell us the whole "why" of society's dark sun spots. We must bear in mind that the Powers are in themselves equally and at all times good, regardless of the uses to which by man they are too often put. To make matters plain, I am compelled to add something in the nature of a revelation. Not in the Powers themselves, but in the DIRECTION, in the harmful using, is it that the mortal has a creation made, has a something into "good for nothing" wrought, made the Devil.

Causes are within, I think you said, and I grant it. Who is so silly as to say there is no mind, that all is matter? Who is so wise as to deny that mind a silent partner is, and being spiritual, works in secret, in the dark, visible only in its objective double?

In social matters all must own the mind's embodiment is a dense materialization. Speeding on its linear way, improvement in productive methods fixes social points. Socio-economic association, the "come by chance" child of industrial planning, has a course of constant tacking, constant tramping. Still, we may reckon on the day of its willingly sought recognition, reaction's blessed work; and then, O heaven-kissed earth, enlightened self-interest coincides with other self in the economic point. Resistance removed, bodies projected by the mortal will continue onward moving in the line of their direction forever. Bodies projected by the Immortal Will overcome resistance of the mortal, will continue onward, moving in the direction of unfoldment, forever and forever.

In this attempt at social outlining, I must of course start from the point named human, from which motions may be generalized as progression along two great lines. As object-lessons help to show a meaning, let us avail ourselves of an instructive recreation. I make a point, and pardon, friend, if I call it human; out from this point I draw a line, not crooked, as you see, but straight; and, as one fiction does beget another (the lesson that we daily learn), so I, bowing to the inevitable, call this straight line the path of the human's intellect. But now I am struck with fear lest you charge me with attempt to perform a jesuitical manœuvre. Not so; at present I'm the sincere follower of majestic, awful example; for are not crooked things made to look straight, and straight things to look crooked, by legislative expediency?

Aside from pleasantry, reasoning, as we are aware, permits latitude, sometimes misleading;

yet we concede that the *general* notion of society admits of precise geometric expression. I am not seeking to deceive; such a picture does not represent the actual social fact. Human dots are in an awful tangle, at unnatural points are pressed too close, at natural points of contact do not closely adhere, and until there is a straightening out it is impossible of them to make a circle, of their doings, impossible to make a square. All things in space by scientific philosophy are reduced to motions. What, you demur? My advice is read Spencer's "First Principles," "go into the silence," on its meaning think and apply. Time and Space, what are they? On this subject the most that can be *has* been said: "two modes of the unknowable." Without doubt it has been proven that things, be they seen or not, are susceptible of mechanical interpretation and of mathematical relationing to the sublime fact, motion.

Time bends to neither side, moves in a straight line, is before us, is behind, for appearance gives no bond.

Space in all directions is, neither comes nor goes, wholly steady, omnipresent, always ready.

To get the ear of Time one lies within its arms; but Space, majestic stoic, is unmoved, cannot be decreased, cannot be enlarged; 'tis the circle divine, the fold of Deity. Time is the line divine; on it we mortals climb to higher views. Point in front of point, spiritual is the motion of the intellect, taking place in time, and yet unseen except by her who reads between the lines.

Returning to our object-lesson, our human dots, patient forbearing things, their rights have been neglected. Well, there were obstacles to be surmounted, but now with willing minds we will bend ourselves unto the work of right positioning. You perceive that, disturbing elements admitted, it is, as I have said, impossible to make of human dots lines straight, lines parallel (geometrics of melody and harmony); impossible, at least, until we've done with social "gerrymandering." By our object-lesson we have learned of two great lines of motion: the mental, and the line of social march. Divine intent would have them straight, and at right angles to each other, but such is not the mortal thought. Still, through an overruling Providence, upon the tramp of intellect socialism has at all times its little, its sure corner. What's the business of the intellect? Well, she's an "agitator," a regular "walking delegate;" into the organism gathers images of things, moulds them into shape to fit the body's needs, and so helps on the spiritual. The method of arriving at conclusions true, after the historic ship has disappeared from view, is spiritual; and if the logic proves not a cystic tumor, but tissue firm and true, with pedigree unassailable, based on general experiences, such conclusions should occupy in literary space, if not a corner lot, at least a favored spot with actual knowledge.

In the earliest, or hunting, stage of society, people roamed in herds, and by preying on their fellow animals clothed themselves and found their food. To this general statement I should perhaps exception make: the gentle, those springing from herbivora, must have been inclined to seek subsistence from the bark and fruit of trees.

In the chain of social progress, could we count the links forged on the line of travel from the hunting to the pastoral state, truthful witnesses would they be found of man's evolution out of a brutal condition. Peaceful dwelling with God's other creatures, thought for them, and kind caretaking must have taught man much, and in fancy I can see him listen to their silent voices, hearken with his soul. Still those pastors preyed upon the bodies of their flocks.

Blest with powers of observation, blest with powers of divination, early folk noted nature, from her took their lesson, for, at divers times and places, from mere scattered seeds they beheld the magic birth of forests — plants and trees. Uncivilized, without legally established authority, the voice of nature was to them both priest and oracle. Prehistoric man, blest folk, free to act, free to think, your mental ear was not clogged with intellectual rust nor parasitic smut; in your social drama there was no Henry Wood to bear the burden of an important part, to hinder progress by his unmitigated "fool talk."*

And so the gentle of those early human kind followed the God lead, broke the solid ranks of ultra-savagery, crossed the Rubicon, and without pomp and ceremony (vain externals, hiding tyranny) took possession of the agricultural estate. Oh! the grandeur of that occasion who can paint? Evolution into humans then and there made possible; people have no need for preying; up and *harmless* doing is the human note. Why so lowly centered, mortal self? Must each step of thy eastward tramp be through hard external knocks?

Become introspective, hearken to the "still small voice." Reason leads to social ways of doing, leads unto a social haven.

---

* In "The Political Economy of Natural Law," Henry Wood says it is a question of Realisam *versus* Idealism, shall the worst or the best be made of existing conditions? Ideal political economy consists in holding up the true potentiality or fullness of what already is. Socialism would smother arbitration, liberty, and discourage progress; consumption would overtake and soon pass production as its practical result.

Dimmed the thoughtful vision which, for existing socio-economic classes, finds by reasoning from the acts of men now living no causative explanation. The earliest conservatives, those loyal to the carnivorous instinct, seeing the peace and happiness of farming folk, seeing their apparent plenty, felt the greed of avarice and envy, and being illumined deemed their " poverty a mere belief," " an error of the mind;" unsentimental, enlightened, "the attractive force of fear" was by them quickly put behind. The sequel, need I it relate? The peaceful farming folk, they who had chosen God, became goods and chattels, and to the unemployed have ever since paid rent. Thus was brought about an interruption big with social havoc.

The natural spread of private property was hindered, hindered was its humanizing work; and unnatural accumulations, unnatural control by the few, have since grown and thriven. Among the many changes that party revulsion brought about was the overthrow of the general family plan, the mother's kindly rule, that social habit of the gens, and, in its stead, politically was instituted the paternal régime and social havoc. Within the organism, plant and animal as well as social, "relics" are found which should have gone with their companions, but they remain to do a freakish, a fatal work.

Everything — thought, event, and state — has its internal and external causes, has its genealogy. There exists in the polite, high-bred society what, from preference, you may call an aberrant variety; but myself, after careful consideration, after profitable reading of learned essays on heredity[*] by him so fond of the antique, am 'bound in conscience to declare the anomaly to be a spontaneous overflow of "germ plasm," descending from the hunting state with continuity as yet unbroken by the civilizer, honest human work. And so it happens that, booted, spurred, armored, these children of wild blood, male and female Don Quixotes, gallop after tiny fox, which from its

---

[*] "Theory of Heredity," by Dr. August Weissmann.

box, by loosening, they have awfully scared. Beautiful their filial piety; picturesque too. Forests and monsters gone and yet equipped and out on view, this atavic variety presents the semblance of dreadful dangers by them to be incurred in a rendezvous with Sir Reynard, or, in lieu of him, an encounter with one belligerent sand bag.

CHAPTER IV.

SOCIO-ECONOMIC FACTS.

THE bond which cannot be broken, try how we may, by means obscure and sinister; the knot which none can sever; the one invulnerable spot, is parentage, relation of effect to cause. To God, the centre of all beings' circle, by whose activities produced, offspring-ing we stand in close relation; yet, from our estate evicted, from natural relation distrained, and by adoption become children of the devil. "La Couvade." Great method!

A fact is that which *is*. The supreme fact, including every other fact, is that we individuals are here upon earth in the equal possession of powers peculiar to our species, and by wants resulting from racial unfoldment we are stirred; therefore we are equally the possessors of the *natural* right to satisfy our wants, to exercise our *human* powers; and anon, when society shall have become human, will come the equal opportunity.

Between equal *possession* of powers and desires, and possession of *equal* powers and desires, be pleased to note distinctions.

The "whence" of our primal powers is "the Unknowable," but to the domain of the *knowable* belongs their "whither." That you and I are on a part of the earth, are in a given social circle, is evidence *de facto* that we belong to the geographical and social portion where we find ourselves to be.

This proposition admitted, then, by a parity of reasoning the geographical and social portion is theirs equally who at a given time are on it and are in it. Accordingly, when in individual instances the socio-economic conditions are less than the broadest possibilities by race progress warranted, then is the inequality due, not to the working of eternal principles which bring us hither, but to social sins that arise from our want of civilization (individualism overcome). Wealth is external nature's gifts moulded to fit human wants by human labor motions. For descriptions of its infancy to the pages of orthodox political economy you are referred, little narratives which take high rank as occasions when moved were those authors by a spirit philosophic. Not suited with its quarters, the spirit fled, leaving their great science unintelligible.

From the individualistic to the social method of production there has been an interesting, one might say an episodal, journey. The family at first was the producing unit, and consumed what itself supplied. The exceptions to be noted are those cases of descent with brutal force applied, evictions and distraint. Simply put, my meaning is, that of wealth-objects there was no exchange. But with stately measure "division of labor" strode on and in time was mated with exchange. The homely mode was barter. Early men discovered that they could trust each other; friendly intercourse was opened up by the act of exchange, and, things being natural, to the exchanging parties there accrued an equal advantage ; each had done the thing to which he was adapted ; prevented was the waste of time and energy. Individual ways were changing as intelligence of things was growing ; growing too were desires ; and thus early folks were led to pregnant changes.

Of a heinous crime I know that I am guilty, am in short worthy of the faggot or the stake, and were this the sixteenth century, blessed with close communion of Church and State, to heaven in a flaming chariot I might be sent for daring to differ from that economic authority which imputes "to man's propensity to truck and barter" the grand social fact "division of labor." It is a slight mistake and no great matter when toying little Freddy gets the cart before the horse, but indeed a grave error in Professor Philosophic seeking to mould the general thought. Division of labor and exchange, twin-born social facts, implying progress in race methods, progress in race wants, do as they have always done — work unseen on social structure their revolutionizing mission.

By act of exchange mutual benefit is derived, be the process simple barter. But *we* are civilized; *we* have money. From a remark which I have somewhere seen a perception may be gained of the present man's attitude on the meaning of exchange : " And these savages use no money, but make presents to each other." Where did I procure this gem ? Well, it may have been, though of this I am not sure, from volumes massive, big with learned lore, dotted o'er and o'er with the dullness of great brilliants; to the Encyclopædia Britannica I refer. Our men, with industrial monstrosities, progeny of mercantile antics, bourgeois economics, are travailing (self-exiled) from repose.

By that remark I am reminded that for social guidance and direction one needs to simply note the act of exchange, and heed its implied meaning ; then individuals would attain an economic equilibrium, repose with peace and plenty.

Ah ! but listen, madame of the moon. With

your men the thought is vastly different; to do a thing so human as to look beneath the surface for a social meaning, why *ours*, by act so unheroic, would deem themselves unsexed. When individual connections through widening variations broadened social integration, then necessity, the ruler, decreed a link between wealth-objects which should be a common measure and a medium of common exchange. In discursive ventures, narrative in nature, one is forced to give conclusions founded upon implied contents of the facts which by them are viewed.

What was the intellectual capacity of primitive men in matters of adjustment, means to ends? Was the application of intelligence ever direct? or was the art of an adaptation the invariable result of an instinctive response to external blind forces pressing upon them? To assert that prehistoric men deliberated and took conscious initiative, is an asseveration faced with scornful look.

This philosophic tyro is groping, feels the need of caution; severe upon men of historic times is its implied criticism; times in which, oftener than otherwise, the birth of great changes comes as the result of a slip, an accident, and, lo! upon the social scene something of full time arrives. But at least this much, without bad taste and without offence, may be accorded: the beginnings of industrial directions, the laying of its *general* mains, was the work of our remote ancestors, those men and women workers of the stone age. And yet "laborers are without intelligence" and they "have no head," says plutocratic authority.

In all periods of time things, and means for their close association, form the substance of society's particular aim. The differences which appear along the line of industrial sequence are in variety and amount, in method and character. The mental transportation undergone must be reckoned among the changes wrought in time. Altered is the attitude of mind. With awe-struck admiration, with terrorized timidity, savage man encountered nature and with her made friends. But civilized man to Dame Nature is impertinent. Facing works of "the Great I Am" early man felt terror, admiration; but, later, men by fearful reverence are stirred only in the presence of their own constructions. Accordingly, untouched by warning notes from the high pitch of industrial methods, bright and scintilating efforts, intellectual and moral, continuously are made to maintain our social maladjustment. In spite of sore corns, the shrivelled, shrunken boot must be worn upon the growing foot; would you have the physical understanding out of joint with its mental counterpart?

The consideration of all classes of phenomena involves that which *may* be seen and that which *must* be seen. The natural onward movement of production called for a helpmeet, for a medium of exchange, possessing, as essential feature, communistic power; consequently into the social drama money came with intent to play a friendly part. Left to herself, no prompter near, the acting would be natural; but interfered with, jerked and jammed about, social tragedy is not unnatural.

Reflecting upon the silent work of common units — weights and measures — the mind is dazed by the magnitude of their service, for by their use not social order only, but all knowledge is made possible. A unique particular is money, offering to philosophic thought an interesting point; for without cavil it is admitted to be a form arising from a pre-existing, a known function; and yet, after all, at its work it is throttled by the wise, the "practical."

In the existing state of industrial co-ordination, speaking from a general point of view, the money thing is an affair of small importance. Bulky things, gold and silver, would in the end but clog the onward social movement. Is it wise, friends, to prop a house condemned? Glad to get the answer "*no;*" but from out the mass such timbers may be taken as will useful prove in that reconstruction which wisdom urges us to set about. Mercantile or individual money exists, though in point of fact it is more "in the mind" than out of it. Token or social money is that form whose intrinsic value is unseen; its use is based on social confidence, and oh ! the game that is played with it. Bankers could a plot disclose, did they choose to startle us by divulging weighty secrets, all the costliness of their paper notes. But born romancers, they prefer to deal in fiction. Could an eagle, however great its power to fly, if tethered to a tree, if controlled by an individual thing, sail aloft and pierce the airy vault of sky? Money is a communistic creature, and from bondage must be freed.

We are yearning for great knowledge. Earthward incline and tell us womenkind, where in nature, true to its guide, you men have found the source of an appearance, the location of an organ out of joint with its official position, and at war with the character of its functional work; why, the thing is monstrous and absurd. Just imagine oxygen, air's life-giving element, frozen, pent up, north or south, and our supply dependent upon the slow gyrations of those poles. "Om" be thanked, our mother nature perpetrates no heinous joke. The people must rise up and snap asunder chains which bind the bird of an industrial growth, the phœnix of an economic past ; and indifferent to incidents immediate and unpleasing, they, with their parents of the immortal revolution, must from their oppressors demand liberty, each standing firm, expecting in the game of chance his freedom through the gate of death.

Treason thus to talk, you say? Well, what of it? Brightly shines upon the road of treason to man's superstitions the star of progress. What about our Declaration of Independence and our revolution? To freely wing the social circle, money must take its source, not at the north or in the south, but at its centre. And now, what says the devil? "Give the gods of society (our laborers) a grand chance to possess the offspring of their toil, the product of their labor motions? *Not if I know it.*"

CHAPTER V.

CONFUSION OF SOCIO-ECONOMIC FACTS. POLITICAL ECONOMY AN IMAGINARY CALCULUS.

A PAIR of social steeds; upon them riders sit, who reach their destination with no exertion other than to goad — rent, capitalism. By the orderly arrangement of society these two racers travel neck and neck; they are beautiful to look upon, they are of high breed, have the same spiritual father.

Rent first in social time God's external gift, bequests to all mankind, did corner; not to be outdone by an elder brother, capitalism plants the flag of *individualism* on quarters none the less divine. Upon the wants, upon the desires, upon the life-blood of the people, this pair of social monsters gorge and fatten. Terse may be an explanation; still the necessities of exposition it must fulfil, else it wants the stamp of utility. To give this stately impress one must dig into the matter to be explained, and must bring into view its internal and external causes; nor until causes themselves have been examined and with mathematic nicety positioned as primary and secondary, is the work done; but then, like unto the solar spectrum, the band of expository colors admits of being gathered into a ray of white explanatory light. The nose upon a face sets all askew; a portrait makes appearances straight and orderly; may be that's artistic, but is the portrait true?

Society is made up of men, women, and our little folks, the children; but measured by the human standard are their relations straight and true? Separation of the inseparable, joinment of that which is forever sundered, is the politico-economic art. How is it done? By wantion abuse of helpless words. Political economy, to these symbols, is a huge abattoir. Its style of putting words together may be helpfully suggested by bits of colored tinsel paper carelessly confused; a prism made, turned, and twirled.

It was fine fun when a child to watch refraction of the light. Unfamiliar with their meanings orthodox political economists unhome economic terms, transport them to foreign shores, requiring them to fulfil impossible conditions, to make crooked things look straight.

For the delusions of this peculiar race there are reasons pathological. By recent exploration the origin is traced to a vile little fellow which microscopists call the microbe sycophancia, but social sanitation is gaining fleet foot. "Labor unions," "single tax," and "nationalism all are working towards the same grand end — socialism. By and by this pesky little wretch, if not dead, will at least be hampered.

An exponent of our socio-industrial creed, an upholder of plutocratic casuistry, defender of economic popery, is "Principles of Political Economy," by John Stuart Mill, himself a heretic. His great soul commands our friendship, but yourself can judge of his mental poise when, as word painter, he attempts the literary picture of our social bog. Wealth, says Mr.

Mill, is not the indulgences for which you have a taste, but it is the sum of money with which you purchase them. After this he tells us that money satisfies no want, that there cannot be in the economy of society a more intrinsically insignificant thing than money, except as a contrivance for sparing time and labor; and with truth might he not have added, the most significant and valuable contrivance with which to coerce the laborer into sparing his comforts and his rights?

At last, after leviathan turns and twists, Mr. Mill lands a *real* definition when he says wealth may be defined as useful and agreeable things possessing exchange value, and upon which labor has been expended. Capital, says this author, is supposed, by persons wholly unused to reflection upon the subject, to be synonymous with money, but money is no more synonymous with capital than it is with wealth. Money cannot itself perform any part of the office of capital, since it can afford no assistance to production.

If reflection plays a logician such a scurvy trick, ought we not for conscience' sake to start in opposition to Christian Scientists? Ought we not to affirm there is no mind?

Labor, says "Principles of Political Economy," is either bodily or mental, muscular or nervous; and we are assured that it is essential to the idea to include those feelings of a disagreeable kind which are connected with the employment of one's thoughts or muscles, or both, in a particular occupation. Though Mr. Mill admits that there are times when muscles and nerves harmoniously combine to perform the body's function, still by implication the marrow of this definition is that nervous matter abides only in the dome of the body palace.

At a time rife with real knowledge, how strange to find a man thinking that muscles moved unbidden by their owner's thought, moved unvivified by life's electric nervous current! Outside the "dismal science," John Stuart Mill is scarcely the man to be accused of knowing only that which is learned from appearances most superficial, so for that strange matter reason can be found, and I think I have it: he was kindly in his nature, his great soul revolted from a social horror—child labor; were their muscles without nerves they could not suffer; thus he stilled his heart's great throb. Oh! the little arms, and the little legs, of little toilers; never do they tire or ache; neither do the arms and legs of grown-up laboring folks.

Have you a kitten? Give a ball of yarn to the little creature, watch him turn and turn, tangled up in the frolic; no occasion for alarm, a straight cut through the mess, so, and pussy is out unharmed; *but oh! that yarn.* Political economy solemnly affirms that though labor may be productive of *something*, yet may it also be productive of *nothing*, which *nothing*, these authors, before the chapter ends, transform into *something*. By the skilful use of their magic wand, and with swearing hand uplifted, they solemly aver that labor is not the creator of objects, but of utilities?

Labor creates not matter, its service to us

is trifling, merely puts things into right positions. Mother Nature is the worker, political economy affirms. What luck! All my life have I nursed a mistake, have gloried in an error, the thought that I knew of at least *one* dame who upon male men had the "cinch" all the time. Ah! Dame Nature, what can ease my sore heart? Political economy dives deep into things, scales dizzy heights, and, when occasion offers, penetrates man's nature; but up and off with more than locomotive speed it breaks the circumference of the living circle. Unmindful that the generic term "man" can be rightly used in argument only to support some general fact, such as a universal desire, a universal want, they, by a tortion movement of being's circle, form a spiral and aid the climb of individual selfishness, of plutocratic spoil.

What is matter? Nothing less than a materializing medium to force, giving it opportunity to demonstrate its almighty might. With spirit, therefore, matter is one and inseparable; it is the same in source. And yet by the thoughtless and the hypocrite how matter is abused. Doubtless on the line of travel it has descended from an ethereal to a solid state. Gas becomes ice, but is not ice preservative, useful? Ask the feverish dying man. Be it so; gross matter then is heaven's ticket of leave; think you that by those celestials such is e'er forgotten? To us gross matter is—well, what is it *not?* It is an opportunity for individualization, the means for an earthly pilgrimage, our donkey ride.

Following the lead of authority to the other half of the socio-economic sphere, let us turn to the department of distribution of social wealth, and here in this sacrosanct realm let us make strenous effort to grasp validity of character in men's interpretation of "the word" to the hewman. Friends, this have I done; I own with humiliation that here upon this mount of superstition, ignorance, and blind folly, erupted by male stupidity, — here reverence for the truth wrings from my faltering pen this admission: that verily there is a spot in space, a niche in time, where persistent labor is productive of nothing, *absolutely* nothing but mental vacuity.

Rent, says political economy (excluding from the definition the disturbing etymological element), is that part of the product of labor paid to him who by the orderly arrangements of society has exclusive (that is unnatural) control over natural agents (opportunities). Let us suppose (this phrase is borrowed from the classics of political economy) — let us suppose this "him" to be unsentimental, in squatter sovereignty standing firm, unwilling to yield a jot of land for folks to live upon, to till. Ah! but payment of rent is the one love charm which ne'er has failed; works a miracle, transforms exclusive owners, makes them sentimental. As I am interested to know what one so mild and gentle as yourself would, under certain circumstances, do, let us suppose that a board was brought, not by a pocket monkey, cute little fellow, but by a big dangerous double-headed gorilla, who, taking advantage, dropped it upon you unawares, and then down upon it sat. That flashing eye reveals your soul, and I am answered: not the time for gentle persuasion, but for motions called forth by the cruel and wicked act, for movements preservative of natural rights, the opportunity to walk free and erect. To dislodge a burden that ought not, need not, be borne is wise and right. God has willed it.

But, friends, I beg you to remember, that which is lawful, that which is just and right to preserve the body free, upright, if done in behalf of the moral self, is not only wicked, but is positively criminal, says male law.

Again, let us suppose that one desirous to perpetuate Herr Gorilla's individualism, an economic casuist, comes and assumes direction of your feelings and your acts, addresses you in this wise:

"Being a common, ignorant fellow, I am come to bring you socio-economic truths and to give you guidance. This position, my good friend, is the result of your own misdeeds, is not caused by another; shiftlessness and laziness bring their just reward. Had you looked out through the back of your head this gentleman could have taken no advantage; that he sits upon your back you have yourself to thank; you refused to use visual agility. No sentimentalist am I, so call to mind your lost chance to climb this powerful monster's back. Does a realist urge you to make known your woes, to make a noise, then is such a one an agitator, seeking to subvert natural social order by stimulating envy, by fomenting dissensions, planting antagonism between yourself and your best friends. By the operation of psychological law, bringing your condition into notice will have but one effect, harden Lord Gorilla, petrify his instruments, the middlemen, turn them into stone. To reach their hearts and soften them by your woes I advise the idealistic plan: keep shady, dark, never let your sufferings and your wrongs be known. Only such should approach you as are equal to the recognition of real causes, *Myself*. Upon your feet allowed, there is possibility of treading more on the heels than upon your toes and then let us suppose the earth should quake. Now the superior position of this creature creates an office ; under social covenant he is trustee, and a double function fulfils ; you are kept from crime, and society is protected from an awful break. To say otherwise betrays hostility to accumulation, to private property, and is an invitation for barbarism to return. See it? What, you don't ?

"The business men, brainy part of society, express themselves well pleased with the style of these remarks, therefore your disapproval I conclude is a personal matter and arises from a desire to arbitrate. I must try another line of argument. With submissive service fulfil thy life mission, my brother ; to toss Gorilla from thy back, upon individual rights thou would'st be trampling. Dost seek coercive legislative interference? Why, impious man, that aim is no better. Endeavor to adorn the position whereunto it hath pleased God to mercifully call such as thou. Be useful, timeserving; peaceably wear this double-headed monster's galling yoke; *yourself* may yet be free. Through natural law this creature's soul by and by with charitable thought may overflow; possibly his benevolent heart may burst. Perchance the precious nectar trickles down this way by thee. Meantime, reflect that thou art dust, and that it mattereth not, at least to us, when thou returnest to the whence from which wert taken."

Reflection with some folks cannot rise superior to the angle of external incident. The occurrence which I have to relate is an episode instructive and amusing.

I was student in the university extension course, that motion which was started by some English women who hungered for collegiate learning. Response to their invitation to come and feed them was by wise men put into form, and there resulted the university extension course, a movement which entertains the would-be student, which diverts the public thought, thereby warding off the expiring groans of those grand institutions of no knowledge but much learning. To the Oxford tutor who through the evening had discoursed upon socialism, had just held us all entranced, this question was proposed by a disturbing element: "Will you kindly tell us, professor, what is the function of the landlord?" Forward I leaned; I held my breath, lest perchance mine ear missed sweet vibrations, knowledge. With calm and dignified composure, with sweet serenity upon a smiling face, the lips were parted and with voice devoid of an emotional quaver the air was pierced (and so were we) with "Why, to furnish land, sir." What need of more to tell? Upon that Philadelphia audience fell a holy chill, for then it knew in what presence it had sat, how near to awful majesties it came; the mediumistic realized that an Oxford tutor, Mr. S., "don of great wit," upon ambrosia had fed, had supped with gods.

You are a tramp. Pardon, monsieur, no offence. I do not mean one of society's best abused, but such man's opposite. Let me see:

as you are inclined to philosophize, and are practical too, I will assume that you are a lover and and a collector of rare delf; are in Japan. The catalogues of various pottery shops to you are brought; here is one representing rare china, exquisite in design, unsurpassed. Hastily you rise, will go at once and feast your eyes, for, if reality be not outdone by an "ad," your soul shall entertain delightful guests, pleasant emotions; but, concluding that it will be wise to make yourself familiar with the location and character of the precious earthenware, you turn again to the catalogue, well pleased with the evidence which it gives of the orderly arrangement of the shop. But this time what do you find? One raving bull set down as ornament.

With spectacles on and with eyes unaided, I have searched a mound rich in fossil treasure, political economy; and here is its explanation of rent. The individuals of society are, by the social phenomenon, rent, divided into two harmonious factions, having a mutual interest in each other. Rent is the effect of a monopoly, but a monopoly which is natural and cannot be prevented from existing. It may be regulated, however, and act as a trust for the community generally. God has given to some more intellect than he has vouchsafed to others, consequently the land is appropriated and held as a sacred inviolable trust for less favored brethren.

It is not known how in society the system of renting was first established. Rent is the spontaneous offering of nature, or an accident. By an accidental occurrence society is divided into landlord and tenant. By this orderly arrangement its individuals are separately classified into controllers of, and beggars for, opportunities to work and live; and by this means the highest possible social functioning power is obtained.

Furthermore, life is shown to be the result of complex organization. Special joints having grown upon the site of the social fracture, society and its atomic parts are enabled to travel economic grounds with a rapid limping gait; and sustained is the analogy between the living body and the social organism, as it is used by political economists.

The land being limited in amount, it is known that a persevering athlete starting from a given point, let us suppose the Brooklyn bridge, and going due west, can, without reversing his direction, if he survive the healthful exercise of walking and wading, return to the exact spot from which he started; therefore are there consequences.

Furthermore, by an artistic use of deductive reasoning (this art no monopoly), it is found that as the spots of land which make up a field differ in their position, therefore must there be an absolute difference in their fertility; therefore, *more* consequences. It is discovered by actual experiment that unlike the *laboring* atom, the little factory child, one molecule of earth-soil cannot be made to do the work of a whole field, of a regiment of atoms. Hence on this earth consequences of no mean order have arisen, which have given a shock to the plans of Omnipotence, and, but for the law of gravitation preventing, they might reach out and destroy the sublime order of celestial space, namely, the necessity to limit population, and the necessity to pay rent. Well-matched, beautiful pair, in you natural selection has done graceful work.

Explanations of rent admit of being arranged in opposite sets, each starting from opposed mythical conceptions, due to the fact that political economists, in their evolution, had reached that point where begin attempts to philosophize.

One set starts the economic Adam from the very topmost peak of best farming land, and as the race has climbed time's ladder downward to more inferior soil, always downward goes the farming man. Like their Maker, ignorant of "the law of population," the. unenlightened economic pair, with superior ground just enough for two, brought forth the family brood. Naturally each one wanted that superior point of land, and so began the crowding and the pushing of brother man by brother man.

This wretched economic mythe, descent of agricultural man, what wickedness has it not begotten? Unmoral thought and act, and social progress impeded. Across the water look. Primogeniture and entail. The family nest legally big enough for only one, and that one a son. The lessons given to Him by men God is slow in learning; other children come, and in the family home by sufferance only are endured.

Somewhere have I seen it stated (I think it was in their parliamentary reports) that the rational, cool-headed Englishman ascribed to the increasing cultivation of inferior soil the rise in price of corn, likewise the elevation of his rent. Then he became mad, not at God, but at his poor mediums, the laboring folk, for taking to their arms the little children sent. Ridiculous, absurd, he argued, and the ocean near providentially provided on either side in which to drown! Fearing beggary from the use of too much land, this orator seriously proposed arrest of the linear extension of land cultivation; no more new farms. In stentorian tones he cried, To benevolence must be imputed the alacrity of those English "land trustees" who enclosed, appropriated the British commons.

To expend thought continuously in one direction is exhaustive; the gray matter of the brain will not stand it; the mind must have a change; so, when occasion demanded, this English orator has been known to declare that, to keep the mercantile value of food up, something must at once be done; stirred by altruistic impulse he shouted, down, down onto inferior soils; stop not; dip in, even unto earth's fiery molten lava; anything, great gods, anything to make hard work, and keep the price of breadstuffs up.

In other directions also the Englishman has strange delusions, relations in the family. Yet I am loth to pronounce him wholly lunatic. However, this is neither the time nor the place to divulge a disgraceful secret.

I have something to suggest before overtaking the theory proposed by good old father Carey. This pious man was certain that capitalism was divinely elected, foreordained; was the predestinated plan; and as he had to own that things were not exactly straight and square, he undertook "to vindicate the ways of God to man," undertook to help Almighty God out of a capitalistic fix.

I speak to Anarchists, they who attack our "Holy Bible." My suggestion is that the next time ye demolish an existing scriptural order, upon God's written word lay destroying hands, ye revise that narrative of our first parent pair and wholesome reversion make. It would have a moral effect to represent the beginning of human travel as an evolution climb, Eden, the earthly paradise, *not* left *behind*, but to be attained by man striving to *help*, not to *hinder*, his *other* selves; attained through deeds arising from the recognition of equal rights, deeds that are human.

To justify capitalism, to demonstrate the rightness of rent, a tax upon the many imposed by the few, Henry C. Carey starts his economic man from the very worst point of farming land; knowledge of its whereabouts, *nil.*

Upon the side of a steep hill, this author says, spots of soil were found so thin that high-bred wild trees disdained to make use of them. Here the Careyian economic Crusoe pitches tent and plants grain, taking care about the depth of the hole ; exactly two inches and no more, lest perchance through the earth-sphere that grain worked, coming up and out on the opposite side, all to the benefit of the "cursed foreigner."

I do commiserate thy hard fate, economic Crusoe, for the antiquarian states that without axe or spade thou didst work. From this, respecting Mrs. Crusoe, we infer——— Was she a gay and frivolous creature, and when not at work upon piano board, were her taper fingers occupied in training bangs, in frizzing her front hair?

Of the necessities of romance our author has an intuition. The success of Crusoe calls up happy emotions ; still I admit that the spirit of envy at the same time is evoked by the greatness of Mr. Crusoe's work. That barren soil yielded plentiful return to meagre planting. Crusoe took the grain, pounded it, and bread obtained.

My head is in a whirl; air, give me air, and let me try to think. Merely from pounding seed, bread kneaded, moulded, and freshly baked came upon the table ready to be eaten. Here, my erring sisters, is occasion for contrition, repentance, for a sin of omission; had men been allowed to do the housework, had they been wisely left alone, we should not now have one chance to mourn a "lost art."

The next picture from the Carey collection is an exact representation of the origin of rent.

I pause to request the reader to bear constantly in mind something peculiar. Political economists know of but a single use to which land is put, that of farming. Indeed, so far behind the spirit and the doings of the time is this peculiar race, that in their presence I for one would not dare to broach the subject of town lots, would expect to scare them off the planet. The beauties and the glories of a picture may be great, but to obtain emotional benefit each for herself must recognize the sublime.

To help us realize the artistic in Mr. Carey's word painting of those ancient industrial doings, whose effect is the undoubted cause of rent, I advise a silent petition to our mental fairy, imagination, to come and help us comprehend his hidden meaning. No longer marshy forests into which, warned by the latest on bacteriology, economic Crusoe dare not enter, but instead an immense tract of equally fertile land. A few families only, holding no converse and having no exchange. In three years, without axes or spades, their unaided fingers and toes raised two hundred bushels of grain, or produced a farm, says historian Carey.

Population was not stationary. God is in it. An overflow of young people; spades were smuggled to them; mermaids (?) did it. *Another* two hundred bushels of grain were raised, or what is tantamount to it, *more* farms were produced. As population increased, more young people, more overflows, more spades, more farms. Natural order at last was interrupted by a man (of such "fool thing" woman is not guilty) appearing upon the scene from ****** No, I will not; please don't urge me; in polite print the word looks ugly******. This man, in the midst of an immense body of equally fertile lands, insists upon having the property of that *first* batch of farmers, and to induce the sacrifice offers them a subsidy and calls it rent; and the record further states that they left to him the whole of their improvements.

Time rolls on, the good work of farm production keeping pace; into use come new and newer implements; anon those landlords are compelled to make concessions unto him who brought occasion for social disorder, brought a cause of moral disease, rent. But woman's be the glory, the renown, of opening prison doors; by bringing death unto the body, she brought freedom to the soul. In the operation of farm production, by the use of spades labor-time was saved; in this lies the nucleus of a great wrong perpetrated, it is affirmed, upon our sacrificing landlords.

To estimate the mercantile value of land, to measure labor-time, to weigh the difficulty of all subsequent agricultural effort, Henry C. Carey exercised his infallible clairvoyant powers upon unaided man's first production of two hundred bushels of grain. Thus Mr. Carey sowed, and thus the politico-economic student reaps a harvest of delusions. From that social epoch until 1878 or 1879, we are assured that all the landlord secures is but his just reward, albeit received vicariously for landlordism's sacrificial deed. There is admission that his share of labor products as an absolute amount continuously increases, but there are protestations that as a *proportional* affair landlords are constantly defrauded, are, in short, robbed of figures. Political economists are ready reckoners, they are mathematical adepts, therefore the two ends of rent's sliding scale are shown to us beginning with 25 per cent of the results of his farming toil, the amount joyfully tendered by that first renter. From then until the time when ended the Careyian reconnoitre, decrease had done disastrous work, wretched landlords being left with about 1-200,000,000,000 as their share of figures, a beggarly pittance truly.

Mr. Carey accuses society of base ingratitude to men who manufactured under difficulties, when, as he says, it was hard. The debt we owe them, he makes out to be incalculably great; does it through a form of reckoning at a compound-interest rate. To their abstinence from eating that two hundred bushels of grain do we owe not only our landlords, but likewise our farms.

Reader, kindly abstain from holding me responsible for the contradiction, for the queerness of this piece of information; remember, I am not the author, but only his word interpreter.

Now this political economist thinks that society should know its blessings, should be honest and not repudiate a debt to legitimate posterity, to lineal descendants in a direct line. I confess that I don't see it as he does, but a thought takes me : that Theosophic theory, reincarnation — perhaps here is an instance for its proper application. Shades of the mighty past, can it be the "egos" of those axeless, spadeless men, creatures called into being by more than Aladdin powers, — can it be that they are with us, are in our very midst, as plutocrats.

I am wondering if Mr. Carey, with Dr. Weissmann, author of "Continuity of Germ Plasm," that theory of heredity which has supplied the possessors of the titles F. R. S., M. A., B. S., and M. D. with food for serious thought, with solid matter, — am wondering could it be that they were "masters" disguised, and had left a distant star to bring to us ignorant mortals transcendental knowledge ? Realizing that the uninspired with inspiration make sad work, I refer my reader to the Carey books, where harmony of interest between the capitalist and the laborer is positively affirmed, not through a point of economic sameness, equality, but through a point of difference. Take note, harmony is produced through a cause for dispute. Those *wicked figures!* While the capitalist and the laborer both get a continuously increasing share of the things which are by labor produced, the laborer, this author avers, gets the best of it in figures; and he allows that this additional advantage should make the laborer contented and happy. But somehow it doesn't.

Stop a bit; I find that I have been too hasty; this page has a new "goody." To make that which Henry C. Carey has declared exists, to make harmony of interest manifest itself and work, invoked is the strong arm of the law. Political protection, adequate and certain, must prevent the consumer from moving from the actual spot where his breadstuff he obtained; this our author is sure and certain will make things straight and square, *at least with the ground.*

"All things come to those who wait." I was on the eve of discouragement, thinking myself ill-used by a long and fruitless search; at last I was made happy, had a surprise; at last I detected a political economist with a conception of reciprocity, a perception of equality in mutual relations, and all alive with useful ideas of how to make society's work natural. I was exuberant, felt that now I could claim the honor of making an addition to the store of philosophic, to the store of zoölogic knowledge; for had I not discovered the law of natural selection in the very act of supension? had I not found in this politico-economic author a variation from and in his particular species? But the thing that puzzled me was *what did it;* not the environment, for acquired characters are not transmitted.*

Henry C. Carey called upon the legislature to interfere and by protection prevent a wrong. The consumer must not become a tourist, a criminal, this pious writer said; no plot of ground should be defrauded of its natural manure, that refuse which resulted from con-

---
* See Dr. Weissmann's "Theory of Heredity."

sumption of the particular grain which the plot itself had afforded. This economic " Toddie " " wanted to shee the wheels go wound."

CHAPTER VI.

CONFUSION OF SOCIO-ECONOMIC FACTS. POLITICAL ECONOMY AN IMAGINARY CALCULUS.

(Continued.)

COME with me into that nation which abhors shopkeepers, is itself a shop—into England. This little country has done fine things, but, like our own, has perpetrated acts which put to blush the moral self. Their social earthquakes have laid some of the different forms of tyranny low, but, foolhardy, their rebuilding was upon the crater, and so in that regeneration which awaits society they will have more to burn than we. This nation has by means fair and by means foul reached out in all directions, has even stretched upwards, given birth to saints, one of whom was real, the Earl of Shaftesbury.

This slight tribute paid to one so truly good, so truly great, I proceed to the substance of this chapter, begin a panegyric.

This land boasts of kings and bloody saints, of literary patrons, and of late possesses a real wonder, public schools. More than a century ago it gave birth unto an intellectual giant, a Hercules, who in time became the prince of bomb-throwers; and this is how the murderous attempt was brought about. There had been revelations of entrepreneur atrocities, and the mother-thought of this most Christian nation was stirred. Their blue books tell; in them one finds enough to turn the blackest of black ink into red. Awakened by such disclosures, the moral thought began to work, and this alarmed British law and order.

To quell the rioters one came from out that class who ordain each other by the laying on of their own clean hands; this prepares them for the gospel work, enables them to keep an ear in heaven. By circumstantial evidence, by relevant testimony, by inferences from his words and acts, this minister is convicted of hatred for the oppressed and of love for the oppressor. His brutal soul had no chord responsive to the woes of toiling little children. The heart of the Rev. T. R. Malthus was full of the plutocratic "coo;" but on the Sabbath, Christ's love was upon his lips.

Om, almighty power, to me incline; I would be filled with holy fire; then to my soul's scorn of stupendous iniquity I might give sound, might utterance give to my disdain for Malthusianism; and then I could express proper contempt for the intelligence of its acceptors.

The reverend gentleman threw upon the spreading social thought his bomb, which proved destructive because the people believed, did not discover that it was merely the empty astral shell of *un*thought. By the word "law" they were asphyxiated.

Now less respect for that term, and earnest search beneath it to see if a moral right is unfolded or a legal wrong covered, would be wise and at least do society no harm. Narcotization enfeebles; which accounts for the few sledge-hammer blows that fell upon that booby thing which the blundering call the "law of population."

Stripped of its gauzy covering, interpreted, this is its nakedness : population exists as the result of people dying by foul godly means, but if the business of foul destruction be taken out of divine hands, be supplanted by moral means (preventives), then population would exist as a result of people never being born. Such is the Malthusian theory ; "only this and nothing more." Records which are going down, down, down to inferior posterity, show that the incredible occurred.

The practical, the thinking Englishman was scared out of his wits by just a clergymen's bogey, in his mascot lost confidence, expected population to rise with tidal celerity and press upon his subsistence ; in anticipation he was hungry, he was starved.

The wage-fund doctrine (nothing in it, no substance, is "without form and void") works hard for, supports, is a fulcrum to, the Malthusian theory. To political economy the wage-fund doctrine is both bone and marrow. This is it : every day in the year there is an exact amount of an unknown quantity of the social funds which His Majesty, the Capitalistic Will, devotes to the purposes of production ; observe, the wishes and the wants of the people are not immediately " in it."

Because the Capitalistic Will is coy, given to coquetry, readily converted from a stable into an unstable quantity, political economists affirm that it is quite impossible to obtain dimensions of that wage fund. Reasoning thus : to know the number of capitalists in a country is impossible, and *were* the number known, in matters of production nothing certain could be based upon it, for, owing to circumstances which nothing can control, the Capitalistic Will is ignorant of itself in industrial affairs. Political economy is derelict ; it fails to make mention of the one point upon which this Will is illumined, viz : the direction, through its aid, distribution takes.

The case is plain : knowledge of the wage fund is a blank ; such is the only possible verdict ; but by *their* method of deductive reasoning political economists are permitted to rest upon their want of intelligence the widest and most far-reaching conclusions. What would be the probable result did mechanics pursue a similar course? We are saved; the laborer is unintelligent, heaven be thanked.

Malthusianism protests that, at any one period of time there is not, of the products of labor, a sufficient amount in existence to supply the actual wants of the people or to satisfy their legitimate desires; therefore *a* law of population is at the helm to wreck a portion of the human crew. Apparently one holy man was unacquainted with productive processes, about the human method to obtain subsistence, food, had no thought; seems to have deemed it a case of manna and of grab. Thus equipped, the Rev. T. R. Malthus valiantly sprang to the aid of the defenseless, to the help of the aristocrat, and poured out vollies, not of grape or canister, but words taking damnable shape. *His* the holy mission to minister unto the highborn, to sustain their fainting hearts, and to uphold their falling arms.

Unto the laborer, therefore, thus he spake: In your interests I have travelled far and wide, have been to Ireland, crossed the Channel, and through the grace of God am back in England, am home safe. I have been, I have seen, and I am conquered, am here to speak in your behalf. I find that your class, mainly through perversity, prefer huddling together, and are ignorant of the land's limited capacity to hold numbers. When open fields are all around, when there is the broad country, why betake yourselves to close quarters? With the sea on either side such a course is reprehensible. I advise you to work nights, be industrious, plant piles, become ocean-dwellers. Furthermore it is laid upon me to rebuke the style of your manners; they are coarse, set at naught noble example, the culture and refinement of a manorial lord. Now, why don't you keep yourselves like gentlemen? Unto me has been revealed the cause of your biting poverty, of your galling want; and as an obedient servant of the Lord the source I must make known—solely your own fault. Too many in Christ's vineyard, redundancy, excess of numbers. Though the Lord hath given you powers, yet their use offends my lord. Your children's hunger presses upon subsistence, prevents the kennels of my lord from increasing. My lord would have his own, his heart is sore; obey the mandates of the Lord, submissively take up the yoke; it is easy, and the burden, let us pray that you may find it light. Cut down your numbers until they are an exact fit of the wage fund. What that is, and how to be reached, lies, I am aware, in a London fog. Precise knowledge is not the forte of my set. The wage fund *does* exist, you know. In successful efforts to find out about it lies the scheme of your class' social salvation. The English laborer is not a "blooming idiot," does not expect through the works of another to attain unto an earthly heaven. Besides, in another direction lie the labors of your betters; they are working to bring about for you the opposite social state. Your numbers diminished, and the size of the wage fund remaining just the same, it is plain that each existing laborer must through the natural movement of economic funds receive his *pro rata* share of that surplus called into existence by his abstinence. What that share would be depends upon division. There are times when knowledge of mathematics would be well, but as a rule it would not help the laboring class meekly to fulfil the station whereunto it hath pleased God to call them. Care has been taken not to blunder, not to sin against ourselves by permitting them to have good schools; they would spoil our servants, make them restless and to us unprofitable. Who says that we are Bushmen? We are Englishmen of the first half of the nineteenth century. I bid laborers hearken unto God; the voice is heard, but needs an interpreter, and I am at your service.

Uncover heads. Thus saith the Lord God: It hath repented me the giving unto the laborer powers of reproduction equal to those bestowed upon the aristocrat. In relationing your kind unto the earth, Omniscience committed a mathematical blunder, to correct which, from heavenly quarters scourges are sent upon you—war, crime, famine, evictions, pestilence, licentiousness, vice, misery, and disease. These, I, the Rev. T. R. Malthus, have named the positive checks to population. Now credit me, if you please, with the great discovery of the Christian era, God's mode of dealing with the recreant class who exercise the powers Himself hath given. Indeed I am not done; I would incite you to a filial deed: head off your Heavenly Father by moral means, by preventives; do not marry; children then cannot be born. Socialists proclaim that men are free and equal, born so; sheer nonsense, you know. Such doctrine is subversive of law and order. The phrase is pretty, to be sure, and upon occasions useful; acts as fuel to keep the party warm in a campaign attack. In a country's constitution it looks well, and from the pulpit it is full of meaning. Still it is mere fancy; nothing practical in it. "Hinds," peasants, the equal of myself or my lord of the manor? Not a "bloody bit of it." Socialists are "blooming idiots." By natural right the products of your toil your own? Another monstrous theory; stirs up strife and envy, turns you from the narrow path, and by preventing humility hinders your upward movement. Take away submission unto wrong and tyranny, what is to call out pure white thoughts? what is to uplift the laborer's soul? Samson-like, socialists would pull down the bulwarks of the temple— of society—and would keep you laborers out of heaven; heed them not; turn to us; believe and live. If there is a thing that makes me furious, fills my soul with righteous wrath, it is to find the laboring class claiming their own. To want natural rights is unaltruistic, is selfishness — in the proletariat.

Unregenerate, would you falsify your Lord, evade the curse pronounced in Eden? Listen: by the sweat of your brow, by the toil of your hands, others all the days of your life shall live and eat. Still ye doubt, are not converted to the truth, but are wavering in the belief that ye press upon subsistence, that ye make times hard, and are the means of raising rent. O stiff-necked, perverse race, why so obdurate? The intelligent, thinking class were convinced before the words of wisdom were fairly out of my mouth. An object-lesson will serve to make plain the injurious effects upon society of an increase in your numbers. Bring me chips; while I hold this one, place beneath it each of the others in succession. There, by such arrangement two obscure events are made plain, the downward movement of land cultivation, and the rise in rent. Increase of rent arises, you perceive, from an elevation of the Adamic farm, fresh strips of cultivation being slipped beneath, naturally it moves upward, and along with it goes rent, "you know." Science makes the duty of the dependent (?) class plain; curb your passions, your desire for social joys stifle, for together this twain must go down and out. Thus saith my lord: Not for you are babies' smiles and babies' love, the child's help to climb; these are for your betters; they must exercise their powers, and the world, "you know," must be peopled. Upon the sacrificial altar bind yourselves. The Lord loveth a cheerful giver, delights in slaughtered lambs; believe and live. God so loved the world that he gave His only begotten Son that men might not perish, but have ample opportunity in which to hate and rend each other, have, in short, life everlasting. Stop a bit; I may be hasty; to compromise is possible; man is not ungenerous *by nature*. As an agent for the plutocrat I offer you easy terms. You must not allow your little ones to grow up, and British laws shall be made holding you responsible for dereliction in your wives, should they, during the three score years and ten, fail to provide them with breast milk. These conditions, while affording your class ample opportunity for domestic joys, will protect the subsistence of my lord from objectionable slaughter. You reject the terms, proposing to trump my partner's ace, beat us at our game? It shall not be; I protest; God intends "hinds" humbly to follow lead. I will besiege the throne of grace, enlist the Universal Father in our plutocratic cause,

O Thou, Maker of the heavens and of the earths, *our* Father, from thy distant abode draw near, vouchsafe divine aid to a conspiracy; we want social order, *our* peace; want to be freed from this talk of equal individual, talk of inborn natural, rights; wilt save us from social heresy? O thou Omnipotent, Omniscient One, in whom dwelleth not the possibility of error, neither the shadow of a wavering turn, have I thine ear in which to modestly unfold a scheme? Unto the laboring class, winged by the lightning of Omnipotent desire, do thou send thoughts of humble obedience, convict them of their duties unto us. Seemeth it well to foster within their minds the hope of an equality in heaven? Then mayest Thou do it; but, Lord, grant my righteous request; help us to keep this class our profitable servants forever and forever. To secure this, our hearts' desire, is there sure way known to Thee? Why, then, send Thine emissary unto me; I would be prepared for the work, and unto Thy name shall be the glory.

With an unctuous "Amen," Holy Tommy's prayer was ended.

On Creation's rosy morn, oh! why was I not there to stay the arm of God, bid Him for guidance wait for Malthus, the *overwise* divine? Let us assume that there are institutions which, by religious antics, fill young men with piety, warranted, for a price, to overflow; and now let us suppose that from such a manufactory, which, from want of knowing better, I call a theological seminary, a professor comes and informs us that in celestial regions there is war, Satanic majesty leads a riot, has thrown the Author of being over the "battlements of heaven," and now claims the works of God as his very own.

A pamphlet lies before me; its author, a convert to the Malthusian creed, is a woman. Her intellect was awry, but her soul with moral was fired. Defying social prejudice, bigotry, braving personal danger, openly she brought knowledge of "moral preventives" unto the married poor. Such an act was noble, heroic, and of a true cause was worthy. By helping them to keep down their numbers, she thought to better the workingmen's hard lot. Could they but secure better quarters, could they but pay higher rent, why then in England a land revolution might be avoided. To society this woman's heart is an ornament, but her head — well, of *that*, ample explanation has been made by able critics; they have said, Annie Besant has a *male intellect*.

This is the place for a disclosure, that British secret. Have I your permission to make a few explanatory remarks? Prompted by self-consciousness our early Christian Fathers showed tender consideration to certain impulses: their benevolence, however, was not a universal manifestation, for they lacked the Christ-thought, the communistic feeling. Upon location in the living field depended the color of the impulse, was it black or was it merely sunburnt. Accordingly, what in men was natural and to be expected, and by anticipation provided for, was in women undivine and on occasions loathsome and horrible. The pagan movement to equalize the sexual relation and secure the establishment of that much social right, was by this pious discrimination arrested, for Christians had a higher aim. This obstruction to the progress of the right is accounted for by a change in the mouthpiece of religious oracles. Among the unillumined, among pagans, oracular instruction was often the vocation of women; but among the Christians this performance was purely by pure men. My English brother likewise is self-conscious; he is a Christian, is just as good as good can be to an important weak personage, himself; but then his moral "I" is sore, is weak of sight, sees differences where none exist.

To illustrate: A London court room. The presiding judge is not a Hottentot, is an Englishman. The case? Ah, well, I am compelled to own that upon occasion the wicked patience of long-apprenticed, well-trained English wives does give out, and then unto the common law they turn, to find it a mythe. Plaintiff is a woman, a wife. Defendant, her husband, not defiant, but happy and complacent, for *he* knows. Unto the lady the judge turns and with surprised tones inquires the nature of her charge. Thinking his ear had belied he repeats: "*Adultery?*" She bowed her head. Confused, the judge asked a superfluous question: Did he deny it? The answer was a stifled sob and an outraged look. Well, really, madam, in the manners of a high-bred English gentleman am I wanting if I venture to inquire what at the hands of *our* common law you seek? Divorce? Incredible; that decree in favor of a woman, and the charge merely adultery, would reflect upon the justice of past sex administration, would establish a far-reaching and a moral precedent. This court is not profane; will not by such decision set at naught the teaching of the Church, commands of Christ.

He suffered not a woman to usurp authority, to tell her husband he should not commit English adultery. Can it be that English wives have lost their piety, turned jesters, gone mad, and, because of wounded feelings, would trample upon their marriage vows " for better or for worse," would, to gratify mere pique, cast out a loving husband, separate a father from his children, and rend the family circle? Why, the thing is positively absurd. The judge's charge is to the woman: Such resentment, madam, is, to say the least, unwomanly. Have you read Gladstone? It would be well to make this occasion a means of grace. To invite oppression is becoming in an English wife; meek submission unto wrong is womanly; nice is the symmetrical relation between tryannous oppression, uncomplaining endurance, and beautiful uplifted thoughts and feelings. The pious spirit is glad of any chance to reach upward unto heaven, even though it be through her husband going downward unto ****. Case dismissed; nothing in it but a woman's whim. Monstrous! Why, the husband was not guilty of cruelty. *Next.*

And again before that judge stood man and woman; positions were reversed. And the lady was veiled. The charge against your wife? Adultery? Did she deny it? Indeed, your honor, that she did, but I have undoubted proof. Crossing himself, after a mumbled prayer, the judge commands the sergeant to light the incense, to bring him holy water, and thus ensured against the contagion of a moral leper, he addressed the man: Wronged husband, whose purity is fouly besmirched, take from the common law redress, an unlimited divorce. Upon men the marriage vow is not a pressing bond; his the right to rend the family circle. Take the children.

Who denies that nature, on the ownership of child, her will declares by a sovereign fact, gives us the holographic testament, but by La Couvade we contest the will, declare nature to be of unsound mind. Nothing is absurd if men so decide. The court would have English wives to know they are not living in times or places of gross immorality, where the laws recognize a woman's equal right to commit an equal sexual wrong. Then with sympathetic mien the court turns unto the demoralized husband, and in hurt tones speaks thus : We men by the injury you have sustained suffer loss of dignity, for when an English wife commits adultery she criminally invades the man's domain, encroaches upon the English-man's prerogative ; therefore, unto you, our damaged brother, the court cheerfully offers, in addition to divorce and child, the friendly balm of sympathy.

Hm ! why is it that the quality of English male adultery is so superfine that British law stamps it as the English wife's perquisite ? For a magician, not to far-off India need we go. The Englishman's thought can potentize a vile thing, can change it from gross matter to pure essence, spirit. What a pity that the operation of this power of magic transformation is limited to just the English *man's* own bestial acts. But this purity is found to be a bother, because to match in bulk and weight the coarse product of civilized countries, British mercantile sense compels something more to be added—a bloody nose or two black eyes—English cruelty. Measured by the principle of equal natural rights, the adulterous law of the most Christian nation is found to be incestuous, befouls its parents, and is a breeder of vice. I do so love to get at causes, knowing that they are always present as external and internal.

Hm! what can be the reason for such adulterous difference? Can it be wholly metaphysical— the "big head"? But this explanation brings knowledge only one step nearer; the puffed head is now to be accounted for; its external and internal causes are to be searched after. Beginning with the cause we know the most about, our first search is for the external reason of the Englishman's metaphysical condition, and its resulting sex-thought. Schools? Well, hardly; too recent is this opportunity for the great English majority whose chance for an education depended formerly upon the workhouse and

God's vicegerents, the clergy. No, the cause, whatever it may be, arose not from an education. The Church? What! that institution which *exhibits* divinity, which embodies and expresses in its works the Christ principle?

Why, before I can go further this must be looked into. As it is my habit to reduce everything as far as possible, make of it an object-lesson, in order that my mind may be by the help of eyes or ears aided, you will, I am sure, excuse if I proceed along my customary lines, write the statements out in full and then compare.

According to the Christian Church, Jesus said, I suffer not a woman to teach. I — suffer —not—a woman—to—teach. That's astonishing! Now, did Christ want His freedom hampered? I can't believe it. According to the Bible Jesus said, Do ye unto others as ye would that they should do to you. *This* has the true ring. But these two statements I cannot correlate. The Christ principle and its opposite do not meet in fraternal embrace ; water pure flows from the skies, not water muddy. Besides, I something know of the Christ principle, and am sure that to impertinent interference with equal rights it does not prompt a body.

The Bible may help me out of the difficulty which the Christian Church begets. As I thought, not *Jesus*, but a *man*, one Saint Paul, did that tyrant-talk, calling himself the true apostle of the Lord. To have grasp upon general principles, to feel their meaning, is indeed joyful, gives unto one a certitude of truth, prevents being driven off by just a puff of wind. But tell me how it happened that the Church got so befuddled, confusing the teachings of Saint Paul with those of Jesus Christ; instead of standing up erect it prefers to grovel, to go upon all fours.

The matter is beyond my ken. My intellect is woman's; now, had I— But, no, I'll not repine, not long for a brain of that kind; for my use it is too heavy. Of one thing, though, I am sure, comparative sociology shows that men have in sex matters made grand progress, have evolved in brutal doings, have the male of our four-footed friends outdone, put to shame their muscular intellects. In all *Christian* lands women teach, the schools are full of them, and yet Saint Paul forbade it ; but necessity is impious ; and then, too, women by Christian men are gotten to do big work for very little money.

Saint Paul tells us, When I was a child, I spake, understood, and thought as a child, but when I became a man I put away childish things. In proof of this I further quote : Judge in yourselves, is it *comely* that a woman pray unto God with head uncovered ? Now, my Christian sister, have you heeded this injunction ? Came the spirit upon you unaware, ere lifting heart in silent prayer,—say, did you run and get a bonnet ? With awful fear my lips are sealed ; I have sinned against the Holy Ghost. " Braided hair !" But, then, braided hair in hot weather is comfortable. To go with heads uncovered the men by Saint Paul are commanded, in order that the image and the glory of God may be seen.

Shutting our ears to the utterances of the

Church, closing the lids of the Holy Bible, let us turn to the " profane " works of the Almighty. There we find the glorious sun and stars; there our souls drink in the moon's serene beauty ; and there we behold walking miracles, women and men accompanied by near kins-people, dumb hair-clothed creatures. Indeed, I am convinced of the relationship of all. Still, in some we find persistent evidence of a close tie — hair upon the human face. Is not that indicative of the character of our descent ? Our brothers betray the species' highborn ancestry ; they bear the family crest.

Women, come, let us atone for past neglect ; in every park, in every home, unto Saint Paul let us rear an altar. Listen ! Aged women are to teach young matrons to be sober, to love their husbands, to love their babies, to be obedient unto a man, and to keep house. Now, I appeal to your sense of gratitude, can anything less paltry than an Eiffel tower bespeak our thanks for that, our " header." The thing that pleases me is to be told that which I already know ; as now to get food into my stomach by putting it into my mouth, or if I would look upon the sky, outward and upward is the veiw.

To Saint Paul men ought to be more than thankful, for if in themselves they are incapable of calling out the friendly feeling, the wife's loving thought, then our affection they all owe to that dictation.

And the little children, what must have been their lot before this true apostle rose? Nature unto the cow was kind; instinctively this mother cares for her young. No need for a Saint Paul to come to *her* guidance.

Much that seems obscure I comprehend, but I own to being "beat" by this particular note of his instruction : teach the young women to be sober. The fact is, I gauge the probable conduct of girls by that of my habitual associates.

Wives, submit yourselves unto your husbands as it is fit in the Lord. Now, as my sex have ideas which in individual instances differ as to what *is* meet and fit, Paul in the performance of his duty was remiss ; with this gospel legislation a recipe was needed. As it is, we women, for all time, are by him left without exact knowledge. You see, *he* knew that in Eve we had a real mental start, for he said that if women *will* learn, let them ask of their husbands at home. If a courageous wife willingly faces the almost certain danger of a disappointment, attempts the heroic by obeying this mandate, now, don't we know the result?

Paul's field of work appears to have been among women, and with the instinct of a politico-economic writer, he tried to eliminate disturbing elements from his calculations. I wonder why he was *divinely* called to the mission. Those Eastern women, I expect, bothered poor Paul, belittled him by their questioning. Naturally enough this *exact* pattern of Him who taught divinely, taught equality, got mad, and to get square with those women sat down upon the whole sex. Pathologists profanely assert that Paul was an epileptic, and so account for his visions ; but this does not explain the delusion of the people who take the apostle at his own estimated value, and who confuse his teachings with those of Jesus Christ. Be ye followers of *me*, he said, even as *I* also am of Christ; and to the very letter Saint Paul is obeyed by the men.

Were those epistles anywhere except in the Bible, had I met them in political economy, I should account for their apparent disorder on the ground of the author's want of perceptive power, his inability to examine into the nature and constitution of the ideas he was putting forth; this, together with unsurmounted difficulties of the English language, would, I think, make the matter plain. As it is I confess my total inability to grasp the Christ drift of his inspired logic: Do ye unto others as ye would not that they should do to you. Modesty is comely. Am I wrong when I say that the gentle Jesus practiced, sanctioned it? But did delicate, refined emotions stir the soul of that pious anarchist, Saint Paul, who sought to destroy for all time the freedom of my sex, sought to obstruct the expression of the Christ principle, natural equal rights?

Admitted, that neither in the existence of schools, nor yet in the teachings of the Christian Church, has the *external* reason for delusions, for the Englishman's weak sight, been found, then further search I realize is futile, and turning, pay respectful court to external cause's mate. Let — me — see ; to give the *in*ternal cause for the series of phenomena which results in British law stamping English male adultery as a thing of fine quality, I find to be impossible until I shall have had a season of communion with my higher, my intellectual self.*** From biological facts, from the workings of life power, I draw data for the inferences I now place before you.

Living matter at first contained within its circle both of the sex principles — sexless, if you choose to call it so — and the method of reproduction was by division of the mass, or by the throwing out from itself buds. Later on came the sexual revolution, divorce was granted, and the separation took place. To serve a special reproductive purpose, the male principle was put out from the general protoplasmic mass. Now we know that an impression may be too indelible for the waters of all time to efface. Filled with a sense of that first impulsion, my English brother feels the origin and the function of his sex.

Reader, I am in the mood to soliloquize; would you avoid a shock, quickly close the book, otherwise ———

Speaking from a general standpoint, is society the better or the worse for the moral teachings of the Church, for the *un*moral doings of our ministers? For, to keep women down to church drudgery, to keep them out from an equal share in the awful doings of majestic synods, is there a wire *too* dirty or *too* rusty to be by "God's servants" pulled? I think not. Ministers lack knowledge of the simplest intuitive truths. To a whole they do not know the position, the relation, of its two halves. Oh, pshaw! that ear they keep in heaven is stone deaf.

Once there was a time when by the word

"minister" my thoughts were led astray; I believed it meant a man divine; but by facts my mind has been corrected.

But where is it, I wonder, that just one little word does sometimes with a woman's life make sad havoc? There are many stars in the politico-economic sky; some are so fixed in asininity's way as to be beyond the reach of my critical telescope. Reader, *you* may possess a better instrument; try its powers upon philosophy of wealth and its near kinsfolk. Economic journals are plentiful, and the glittering rot abounds. Is your leisure small, and the wish to conserve time great? Then I advise selection of an economic essay by a university professor; at once you are admitted to a full view of the grotesque and clownish show. The authoritative books upon political economy have been written by men who were under the impression that the object of professorial effort was to divert, amuse, and entertain college boys while their mothers were at work. Such are the pets of the university. It makes a body think of poodles and of doting dowagers.

"Postulates of Political Economy" soars high; sees no natural tie between an image and its reality. Its major premise is an assertion which the author himself assures us is empty, but under it he places minor propositions, social facts, and his own wise conclusions, and of course he makes them fit. To blow bubbles, little sonny would at least put soap into the water.

Then there is that distinguished thinker, a mathematical lunatic, whom the Encyclopædia Britannica accredits with sagacity and ingenuity, fixes him in literary space as the possessor of a bold and scientific imagination. By referring you to Prof. Jevons' books, I perform my whole duty, but instinctive humanity prompts me to caution you against a shock. His mathematical prodigies are all of them monstrosities. The labor which brought them forth was instrumental.

"Plutology," a wonderful mess of words! Sometimes in a name there is much misleading. I thought I had found something new, but no; it proved to be the same old story of the regulars. Statements are moved about, some are brought to the front, while others are placed in the background; as a housekeeper, by rearranging her furniture, might give to the room a new appearance. From the conglomerate, where the author talks intelligently about the poor, their crimes, the way in which they are ill-treated, their wretchedness, their sufferings, their squalor, and their helplessness, society's neglect, voluntary idleness and inability to get work, their woes and their wrongs, I selected this very funny thing, which looks to me as if it were intended for a covert or half attack upon the good old Queen. The argument was that when she gave her wealthy children bread she ought to be allowed to give something to her needy offspring. Rambling in the woods, when a little girl, I got lost, turned completely round, and started for home in the wrong direction. Do, please, wont some one fit out an expedition and rescue that man Hearn? "Let us assume" that he is not a learned professor, only an empty LL.D.

As to the book of M. Bastiat, his work from beginning unto end is one prolonged hysterical yell: My property, right or wrong! my property!

Before directing my telescope to the luminous body I have now in mental view, I must, as a careful physician, request that you will, by veils or bits of colored glass, protect the sight. William Senior, of Oxford University, was much hampered by the paucity of the English language, bitterly complained of political economy's defective nomenclature, while giving to his readers ample opportunity to deplore his defective use of the same; words, words, words. This professor was full to the brim of them—word obesity. His case is about the worst unrecorded. Had I been called to him, I should have put that mouth in plaster, should have reduced him to the practice of mere gesture, and think I might have worked a partial cure. The English peasant, it is said, commands a regiment of only about five hundred words; had he taken the science of political economy out of the mouths of university professors, what needless word-slaughter had been saved!

Prof. Senior, in dealing with productive and unproductive consumption, makes things plain; informs us that the third footman to an English carriage may or may not be, on the part of the owner of the equipage, a piece of unproductive consumption. Which it is depends upon something of which Prof. Senior is not sure; but he was certain that what the footman consumed was not bread and butter, but was his wages. Aged folks, this learned man found, from the standpoint of his great science, to be permanently unproductive, but of the infant's future usefulness he had permanent hopes. By careful searching this political economist discovered this alarming fact, that the number of absolutely productive consumers was decreasing, as decreased the social black spot, chattel slavery. Prof. Senior thought it probable that in time the sole cause for consumption of food will be hunger and the body's demands, and that no one will eat just on purpose to satisfy the commands of a legal owner.

Profoundly impressed is this erudite by the *real* defect in a sale, say, of an English mansion. Long past pleasurable emotions of an owner do not accompany, do not make a part of the transfer. But suppose the seller a melancholic, would the buyer be the gainer or the loser by this ethereal defect in the transfer? His keen perceptives enabled him to readily grasp long past situations; he avers that at first there were only rent and wages; later on, with civilization, came profits. The fairy which worked a miracle, transformed a little star, twinkling in the darkness of a far-off institution, into a luminous body, was the theory of abstinence.

This theory, like much that political economists cast off, may be set down as due to the whirl of two fiery opposing mental currents. Society being divided into controllers of and beggars for opportunity to work and live, profits take the wrong direction, do not get home. But an economic prestidigitator writes a treatise and by assertion proves that right is wrong, and wrong is right, and as a result socio-economic blackness is turned white.

As wages are the due reward of labor, so profits, which the plutocrat receives, are merely proportionate to sufferings entailed by abstinence, says Prof. Senior. Now, where is the fancy that can paint the terrific soul leaps, agonizing pains, horrible sensations, which make good the title of our *entrepreneurs* and our bankers to all that in the form of profits they get. As with revelation I fear to "monkey," I think it best to take up bodily and transfer this author's own words. Abstinence is realized instantly in the conduct of a man who allows a tree to grow or a domestic animal to come to maturity. Dear, dear, what a pity! Had he added, "and permits his wife to stand up straight," the world would have had a finished picture of Professor Senior's complete asininity.

I own to seeing much of the animal in men, but "'pon my soul" I have yet lengths to run if I catch up with William Senior's slander. Among the men I have friends; man is not a mad bull; I deny it. Still, I own that he is the child of his adopted father. Especially realizing exactness of nomenclature and strict accuracy in deduction, his new term "abstinence," though useful, was not appropriate; his treatise is of a high order. So says the jargon of that article on political economy in the Encyclopædia Britannica.

I have an incident to relate before proceeding to the classification of political economists. One evening in Philadelphia, at the close of a discourse, questions to the donor of the intellectual manna were proposed; this was usual in the university extension course. It had been claimed that what was wanted to smoothe the social waters, make our crafts skim along easily, was simply intelligence in the laborer. Disturbing elements abound; need I remind you that anarchists, socialists, and single-taxers are on hand wanting to get at truth, wishing to see things righted, popping up on occasions when not wanted. This time it was a socialist. As a babe longs for milk, so longed she for knowledge; therefore to that professor she meekly put this question:

"With a definition of intelligence will you oblige us, please?"

"Intelligence, intelligence," he said, and there were signs of wildness in his manner, —"why, madam, intelligence is intelligence."

But, unsatisfied, she persisted in questioning, insisting on his going into the matter deeper. (Professors should use caution against the bombs of bloody socialists, be protected, armored by the power to answer simple questions put.) An awful retribution came nigh being hers, that of sending forth a spirit unprepared. I was present, saw the question's toxic effect, and knew the imminent danger. With Christian Science methods at once I came to the rescue. "There is no death, there is no death, there is no death," with fearful energy *mentally* I shouted, and was rewarded by seeing slow return into that face a look, which, through the paucity to which I have referred, I am compelled to call intelligence; and he survived.

I have waited, and have looked for the

notice of a university raffle, but no, the Quaker City is still illumined. Now, were my opinion asked as to his natural location, from recent revelations I should without hesitation say, the University of Chicago. What a tandem team that institution would possess! Prof. Batting does not know what intelligence *is*, and Prof. Harper does not know that intelligence is to be *used*.

To possess diamonds or pearls some one must dig or dive; motions to discover, to own the truth are similar. In form and figure mythemakers are men, but in mind they are ———— However, yourself can judge. The earth; upon it a mass of protoplasm. The time, ah, well! I do not know it. Would that I were clairvoyant. And now begins life's journey upon this planet. Encircled within that living mass lies Om, the life power. Alive and beckoning are possibilities, but sleeping are the powers; they by external forces must be awakened, called forth into the tree of manifested life, whose parts are sub-human, human, and divine.

Bear in mind that the topmost bough, the uttermost leaf, are, through the trunk and root, connected with all the rest. Vast is the wealth of this rich matter; the poverty of my perception is to be made plain.

To philosophize, conceivable data must be assumed. Scientists hypothesize an ether. In thought let us try to picture the fact of an unknowable, undifferentiated mass, a universal sea of consciousness (feeling); the Omnipotent, all one thing, everywhere waiting to be built up into mental states; and to the general consciousness we must trace the relationing by the mental principle of its coexistent sum, the environment. The evolution of protoplasm and the maintenance of forms depend upon the reciprocal action of two sets of motion whose points of initiation are opposite in direction, are without and within.

I am not considering the term direction as for convenience used, but am dealing with direction in its connection with the unfoldment of a mass of living matter, which to this earth is relationed.

Thus considered, motions initiated by the environment have for their field of operation the inside of that living mass; but motions initiated by the powers within the living substance, take, through reaction's course, an opposite direction, proceeding to the outside.

Bear in mind that, at present, I am considering protoplasm in its early progress of unfoldment, have not come to where the road forked, where evolution was aided by thought consciously initiated.

The northward movement is a motion of the protoplasmic self, its upliftment into forms, which was a result of the harmonious combination of these two sets of motion, whose initiative points, though opposite in direction, are interdependent. That mass of protoplasm knew at first but a solitary feeling, hunger; other feelings, knowledge, came through an acquaintance with the environment; pressure gave the introduction; a pebble or some tiny thing dealt idiotic individualism its first blow.

In the perception of something outside of self

the mind had its gray dawn, had the nucleus of its germinal beginning ; and as mental states grew in number, in substance, and in form, into existence there came new and newer forms of manifestation. Now, where is the power that can magnify the results of co-operation, of friendly relations? Until a creation had been wrought, protoplasm could not move except as it was acted upon by something outside of itself. Basely born, educed by gross matter, that mental state, the first on earth, stood within the living mass alone. To move protoplasm it was helpless, for it was but a half. Everything in nature has its unseen counterpart, its spiritual portion. The cry for help was heard, and on the wings of echo, from out of general consciousness, came its mate ; and by an immaculate conception that first mental state was made whole ; by a miracle was started the living individual soul, the home of all emotions, all impulses. The environment being large, great was the need of education ; trained assistants came — the senses—brought by repetitive effort.

Nature knows no mistakes, admits no failures. In time all motions, experiences, take some ultimate good form. Within the mental aggregate the will is born, a mental entity, and itself becomes an individual part, helping to make up the body of the mind. As an existence the will is freed from dependency upon the immediate action of external forces upon sentient matter to call it up. It is in this sense that the will is free. But for opportunity to move the machinery of its operations, the body, the will, though self-existent, is still dependent upon the environment. Chain a dog, and for what movements are its legs free? Freedom's lever has two ends; opportunities must be unchained. That mass of protoplasm which had strayed from out of space, landing on the earth, held, with will in its possession, an earnest of its homeward motion.

But the mental embryo, though viable, was not yet ready to be born an infant mind. The nucleus of something more was needed, the germ of the moral self. Behold the mother thought and friendship true in our friends, the quadrupeds. The principle of sympathy works sublimely; by its help base-born mental states become the substance of the soul.

I ne'er dispute that man images his gross maker, but most emphatically I do deny that we have yet attained unto the image of our Divine Creator. To become this, man *himself* has work to do.

The meaning of life-work? Well, I take it to be this: nothing other than the building up of feelings out of knowledge, out of perceptions of motions that are started by what is within and by what is without. The meaning of life-work —is it less sublime than this: the precipitation of states of feeling, of emotions, into individual soul and body?

The vibrations of etymology tell the story; they help to make it plain. Language had its mound-builders, and their instinctive realization of the true relation between ideas and their verbal forms is just amazing.

The power within, which co-operates with

external forces to mould protoplasm into different forms, is the mental principle. And what a worker! Immediate perception of like points, of things, of their meanings and relations, conclusions come by a process of spontaneous generation. Judgments of the mind take form. Into the mental country immigrants are constantly coming; some hail from the realm of thought, are refined; others are gross, they image sensations. Still, there is no discrimination against them as to the rights of citizenship in the mental country. All are admitted on equal terms. The principle of the mind is, as you know, not a brute.

Threefold is the general work of the mental community, for not alone new entities are added, but the process of destruction is carried on. An anarchistic duty is constantly, quietly, performed through evolution's work; old conditions are broken up and old states are transformed, are adapted to new forces; hence there are peace and harmony in that complex society which we call the mind.

Note the limitations. This affirmation is only true of the mind as an existence, a whole composed of differentiated, of individual parts; it is not applicable to the mind's mortal manifestation. Here confusion and disorder may and do arise. When traced, invariably is it found to be due to interference with the rights of, to wrongs perpetrated upon, the mind's materializing medium, the brain. Of the body's parts, nerve substance is the nearest to life power. Look in upon the medium, something you may learn of the greatness of the unseen work; though not much, I own, for nature in her generative work is silent, is secret. Would you really learn, then, the harmonious relations of the brain mass must not be broken by rude, impertinent intrusion, by coarse acts; deathly quiet should invite the looker-in.

To compare cerebral masses is instructive, and so, beside the brain of an Aryan woman place that of an elephant. The soul's sense of sublimity is awakened by the differences perceived; condensation of the mass, smaller size, superior quality. That refinement was effected through intellectual thought's transformatory power. While nature had on hand this work, to build up a brain, an animal, prior to the job's completion, might lawfully claim that larger size, greater brain weight, were evidence, *de facto*, of his superiority. But the finished product upon life's market, then the all-important work of transformation begins, then the main business is to give to that brain a good character.

The movement in textile manufacture exemplifies this fact. Though by stupendous effort the first woven fabric was produced, yet since that marriage of intelligence to art, what has been the direction of the manufacturing march? Why, from bulk and coarseness to smaller size and fineness. It is a question of quality; note the delicacy of gossamer.

Brutal muscles call for bulky brains; natural selection is at work, and great brain weight responds to brutal thought. To review, first, the perception of things, then the perception of the relation of things to self — what as to pain-inflicting was to be avoided, and what as food was to be sought. Later comes the perception of relation between things; reasoning power begins its work. Still the intellect is animal. To dig up causes by the root, their separate force to discover by their separate position, primary and secondary, and by discrimination to relation them to effects, is man's prerogative, is his moral duty. Man's is the work to search for meanings, the "why" and the "wherefore," and by noble discontent moved, rest not satisfied until the knowable is found and expressed. Is a mind's work less than this, then is that mind sub-human. Animals know much, have learned it by experience, still they take things for granted, and they judge from *appearances;* the animal mind cannot do otherwise.

Political economists perceive socio-economic institutions, but do not trace their origin to real first causes; they judge from appearances and treat landlordism, capitalism, as natural to human society.

In my classification of political economists I

am not alone ; I can quote authority. See "The Industrial Revolution," by the late Arnold Toynbee; note his separation of them from human folks — "the bitter argument between economists and human beings has ended," etc.

Variously may causes be classified : those in space into internal and external ; those in time into primary and secondary. But according to their character causes are classified into general and particular. While the *general* cause for this peculiar race is to be found in the confusion of our socio-economic state, the *particular* cause is chargeable to universities, our intellectual junk shops.

Therefore I call upon the women of all lands to come forward and do a great work. By arguments which must take the dullest brains, importune the government to take possession of these institutions by the right of eminent domain, and under the superintendence of an energetic woman, one well versed in kindergarten methods, conduct their future work. By this means a needed revolution will be peaceably secured ;

less professors, less fool talk. Spare no effort, see to it the work is thorough ; but women, "for God's sake" teach those learned men the meaning of the simplest words.

What ho! ye discontented laborers, gods of society, what is it at our hands ye ask? Mine ears do hear "the jargon, natural rights," equal opportunity to possess, to enjoy the things yourselves produce. Spake I unto you as unto laborers, this would I say : Know you not that selfishness is shocking ? From example take a lesson, live at the expense of others, be plutocrats. But interpreting our socio-economic state, I speak to you as unto gods of society. I am not a scoffer ; we are optimistic, in the fullness of your powers have confidence. We are lovers of consistency, and would, in all things, as becometh deities have you to act ; live upon nothing, enjoy nothing, but for your dependent, society, create everything. One thing alone you lack, character ; take heed, build up character. Hearken to capitalistic warning : Go to ; the right of conspiracy belongs to us and not to you.

Myself thinks that even gods have rights, therefore it is with reluctance I own that grave charges against you are preferred, a few of which, just to make myself solid with your adversary, I will name. You are arraigned by the great, by the greatest of great folks, by political economists. The misdemeanor charged, you create no matter, but instead you prostitute your powers, and you spend *our* time in the production of mere trifles, utility and form. I desire in all things to keep steady, to retain firm grasp upon "the straight line," but this unexpected, this astounding disclosure, wâs for my nerves too much; from centre to circumference my mind by it was shook.

Would you cause a fellow-creature's disintegration, cause my return to nebulosity, then continue on in this blunder, continue this omission.

Against your class the list is very, very long; and life, you know, is short—but three score years and ten. Did I attempt to give it all, I should at last be found unprepared to meet death's call. I will be wise, I will curtail, from scientific art take a lesson.

The charge selected is, of all the rest, a composite; in it the Christ-like feature of your reverend friend is recognizable. He differed from Ricardo; declared that capital could become redundant. With this reverend sir, to open mouth and to prove statements was a simultaneous and a wonderful performance. "The distinguished thinker," as heretofore, makes good, by the plausiblest reasons, his new claim. The walk of capital, he urges, is steady, and steady its increase. The social waters are, by him, admitted to move; we are told of an occasional ripple, of a fresh call for new laborers, and, alack! the labor market being *under* supplied, sixteen or eighteen years elapse before the capitalistic call is answered, before the plutocratic demand is fulfilled. Capital all this time is increasing; having no vent it is dammed up. Meantime, until the demand for fresh human hands is overtaken, accomodating witches manufacture goods and chattels, they produce the redundant capital. Sixteen or eighteen years before the scarcity of the labor market is corrected, and all this time, upon the "ragged edge" of suspensive wait, capitalists are kept by the tardiness of a class convicted of redundant reproductive powers.

The case against you "pans out" bad; I own it, and as a friend of the gods I should not like to see this matter fall into the hands of "able lawyers;" consequences unprecedented would arise. Malleability is a property of "cases," and judicial patience is a magnitude. Through *tiers* of courts it would be took, but without a "precedent," without an anchor, judicial labor would in the end prove itself dimensionless space.

The Rev. T. R. Malthus included in the lapse of time between response and the capitalistic call (bring on fresh human "hinds") the period of their gestation. I am *sure* he did; still on so grave a matter I am loth to have the reader think I may have erred. Malthusian gospel is economic authority, "and so it please you" look it up, get at the awful truth. Gods slighted money's call, were years in bringing angels into the labor market. In the affairs of laboring men "there is a tide, which, taken at the flood," etc., etc., *ad infinitum.* In its special application it doth appear to me that the mind of our economic expert, "vicegerent" Malthus, was by divinity potentized until was reached that point in high attenuation's process where supervenes etherealization, hence Malthusian thought went careering up and down, shot in all directions at one and the same time; and hence an exhibit of unified disorder in his ideas.

I more than half suspect that the string which, for a time, tethered that spiritual being to our coarse earth, was his ministerial mission, was his special adaptation for the work of saving souls. As already hinted, the demand by you laborers for opportunities is deemed by us unworthy your high vocation. Examine great society's seal, see the stamp it makes. In the social adjustment affair hew-man's head does not work.

To move the human heart your claim is an insufficient cause. Furthermore, to your godlike jealousy we humans take exception. To aid comprehension of the present state of socio-economic affairs, be pleased to note the wholly materialistic character of the Christian conception. God resides not within the self, but outside; is it wonder then that KING MONEY'S men strive for themselves to corner the spot where their divinity abides? And furthermore, I would have you note that God Himself has to seize the opportunity, has to hew His way.

Our time on earth being limited, we attend not to frivolous affairs; business presses; the claims of God's mortal adversary must, you know, be allowed. Accordingly society's gods have their wrongs, and were they compiled, put into historic form, the stench would burst a vellum cover. In union there is strength. Look upon the living body, see equality in opportunity; in the co-relation of its different parts behold omniscience, each for all, and all for each.

Friends, kinsfolk, society: by permission of the principle of right I come to speak; at your feet I come to lay not Cæsar's wounded corse, but a living, bleeding cause. The "noble" capitalist tells you that the laborer is redundant; it is a "grievous fault;" but methinks the laborer is society's true and faithful friend. Has judgment "fled to brutish beasts?" Has society lost its wits? "Bear with me, my heart is in the" cause. I would not do the "noble" capitalist a wrong; he is an "honorable man." Better, far better, to wrong a righteous cause, myself, and you, society, than to wrong the "honorable" poacher of his brethren's opportunities. With proper reverence for the gods of society were your hearts and minds disposed, then against dishonorable social conditions there would be universal rage and mutiny, and you would do the millionaire-opportunity a wrong.

Better would it be to let the cause of right suffer. The "noble" capitalist hath told you that to the laborer he acts as better half, as guardian angel, spiritual wife. Come, judge of heart-throbs for his beloved; listen to the capitalistic refrain: "Whene'er I take my walks aboad," how many poor I see; "what shall I render to" my MONEY-god for all its "gifts to me?" And now watch the exhibition of capitalistic love. A wolf and a sheep in close proximity together stand. Of individuals there are at present two; but the wolf loves the sheep, would him enfold, would him shelter, would, in short, with him make but one. Moved by this paternal feeling, forward with open jaws upon the helpless sheep he leaps, simply performs the common socialistic feat; and now of individuals there is but one.

Friends, kinsfolk, society, hearken not to the wisdomless science, political economy; by its folly have your heads been turned. Its fathers, seized by a sub-human spirit, prophecied that to increase wages were of no avail; laborers would not hoard, but would squander the golden gift, like as not upon more tables and chairs. In laboring folks this is a heinous sin. But then, society, reflect, be merciful; it is barely possible that a laborer stood in need of an extra table, and mayhap one more chair; maybe he had a guest; maybe he entertained an angel unaware. The gentlemanly capitalist doth tell thee, O society, that the laborer is coarse, ill-bred, is unrefined; and relevant testimony is overwhelmning; verdict is found. The workingman cuts not æsthetic capers; he is convicted. But stay, withhold thy judgment, O society; the power to move thy stony heart may yet be mine. Reflect: from out the inferior ranks the æsthetic star has not yet risen. Consider: for phosphorescent light the laborer is doomed to dependence upon the shooting of a comet across his firmament; doomed to dependence upon a wandering apostle from out of ours, the superior ranks.

Friends, kinsfolk, society, "lend me your ears." Behold the laborer's holographic testament, his will and willingness to do for his dependent, You; and then behold his hampered opportunities. Methinks it is as if the rarest jewel, the diamond's brilliant, sparkling hue, round about were set with pitchy blackness. What does the laborer do for society? Everything; all. And, I ask, can aught be more despicable than taking favors, and for them making no return? I trow not. What can society do for the laborer? Much. Unclasp the exploiting hand. It is upon his throat. Abolish the economic tenet, Your necessity is my opportunity. Of vain pretensions I am a scoffer. Has society an intellect? Use it; despise the needless. Look, perceive the truth of socio-economic truths. Society, for enforced helplessness I thee arraign. From out God-space the infant comes upon this earth, comes to unfold principles and powers, comes to set knowledge in motion. I demand to know why, if born without the golden ticket-of-leave, one heavenly waif should, by thee, be left to starve, left to freeze. And the aged helpless, they who have borne the brunt of battle in past days, and with tottering steps approach the river's brink, I demand to know by what ratio, by what rule of three, thou, society, dost justify the cause of their needless tortures. Socio-economic conditions? This thy plea? For sub-humans such would do, but where there is head and heart, for *thee*, O society, it is inadequate, it cannot bail thee out.

The youth through whose childish day-dreams flitted fairy thoughts of future possibilities of future doings, wonders; upon the threshold of manhood's morning see him all alive with glad courage, with great hope. Why, his very soul feels too big for his mortal body; pitiful the thought, he finds not a thing to do that suits. Pursued, opportunities flee like the mirage, and he is tripped, finds himself ensnared. Society, hast thou a heart of steel? Even then feel this tragedy of transformation. The buoyant youth developed into a disappointed, discouraged, heartbroken man, without hope; mechanically he toils on; wife and babes from worser fate must be saved, if possible. Opportunities are tied up.

Society, earth's omnipotent one, untie the

Gordian knot, prevent the cut, arrest the falling sword. Wicked society, deaf to the cry of thy helpless children, repent, turn from thy paramour, man-thought; break from its control. To the principle of right flee, and to the principle of sympathy be wedded.

CHAPTER VII.

SOCIAL LAW THE ECONOMIC LAW.

LYING within the arms of time, the mental principle moves forward; its unfoldment is onward in a straight line. In space things are positioned to it transversely; theirs is an outward, is a broadening motion, and if progressive evolution be obeyed, then at the point where meets the mental and the line of social transposition, a right angle is made; but does obtuseness interfere, reaction then must work, must make that angle a right one.

That first protoplasm at first moves only as it is moved by wind and wave; later, when internal forces have been wakened, see that creeping thing a worm; conscious of environment it moves intelligently, and we find, later on, time's motion symbolized by a spine, and stability is given to that protoplasm. Fishes, with one exception, have a head and heart ; the lancelet has neither.

Note the combination, my plutocratic brother ; head and heart, you see, belong together.

Leaving that great class of beings, some of whom move gently in their environment, while others, through seeking to bend the mighty eventful current to their wills, lash the sea into a foaming fury, and still following the evolutionary movement of that protoplasm. we find it a vertebrate and upon the land. It must learn to walk ; internal forces must have a better opportunity for unfoldment, it must have a larger scope, more and more of the environment ; no longer easy movement, carried by the ocean current ; that protoplasm feels itself abused, pulled down from a high estate all its own, and disappointed, it croaks.

Nature, weary with dull plodding, for her own encouragement created the birds. And, oh! the eagle, up, up, her feet freed from the dirt of earth, in space away, away, of sublimity and grandeur what must her soul not feel. Once more we find that mass of protoplasm fastened to the earth, but, oh! the earth is grand and good, is willing to be helpful, to aid in the progress of the body and the soul.

Once it starts in individual motion nothing can arrest life-force. The principle of activity knows no cessation. Differentiation, variation, are the natural accompaniments of its tuneful course. Movements along all lines would, from the primal starting point, be progressive but for hinderments begotten by the mortal, the devilish mind.

By ape the marvel was foreshadowed, and the bud blossomed out, and that protoplasm stands erect, is man. Look within; there is a skeleton.

While the evolution of being is from the primal starting point a progressive motion, and while the general movement of society is ever onward, whether in particular instances the social motion be one of progress forward or not, just depends. There is a state of communism, and, willy nilly, all are "in it;" substance and spirit, or protoplasm and force, in the environment.

To live, all animated things must breathe, must drink and eat; and a prerequisite to progress is freedom of movement. You perceive that, to begin with, there is an essential uniformity: but be not exercised, my individualistic brother; variation, by the very condition which so alarms you, is secured. Omnipotence is at the helm; trust it. There is no occasion for an economic Saint Paul.

The environment does its part; there are opportunities, there are supplies. To provide the body with organic means of adjustment, with sense organs, is the duty of internal force. Differentiation, variation, with ghostlike tread follow the main lines of motion, and so within the body there are organs distinct but not separate, co-related by the fact that for the organism each does a useful work; co-related by their mutual equal dependence upon a common environment, the blood supply; and co-related by that environment's impartial, equal distribution.

Each organ just helps itself to what the general fund contains, and *itself* decides *what* is for *it;* be there interference, overloading or congestion of some part, then disease and death result. Soundness of mind, health of body, absolutely depend upon the exercise of equal freedom by all the body's parts, depend upon the preservation of natural rights, of equality. Shocking communism, but which of us is willing to declare it off? Social law is the condition of good management. Would you scale the mountain's side, then to your aid the plane is inclined. Blessed uniformity, were thy smiling, peaceful face oftener seen, welcomed by society, great conservation of energy and great progress would be made.

" Let us assume " that there comes unto our new-born man, from out celestial space, an avatar; tells him that through struggling against the needless ignorance, and through work, there will in course of time come a manifestation of great advancement by the human folks; tells him that where dense forests rule supreme, where he, a naked savage, stands, cities shall spring up, that folks shall dwell in houses, protected from the wind and rain, and, though unacquainted, shall live together in peace and in harmony; that people shall go dressed, and in that future men and women shall travel, not on foot, great distances; shall skim the mighty waters, not on icebergs, but in houses propelled by imprisoned steam; that food to be eaten shall be cooked, and that about its condition folks will evince some little nicety, some cleanliness.

Look quick! That savage leaps into the jungle, and hark to that shriek: U-TO-PI-AN.

The gentle god within that savage soul had not her wings unfurled; unconscious of the "still small voice," but conscious of the brutal wish, his answer was but natural. Construction results from the relationing of parts according to their natural condition of adjustment; be this rule despised, conceive yourselves, is it possible to have a house or a bed? That alone is natural which bears the stamp of Om, which springs from the inherent constitution of a thing, from its essence, spirit; conceive yourselves, is it possible to convert pine into cherry wood? Biological records silently say that inconceivable ages passed before the mind became an entity with force sufficient to the construction of the human form, but since the occurrence of this formation in structural life, inconceivably great (along some lines) has been the mind's advancement.

This progress has been occasioned by the perpetual onward motion of perception, how to relation parts, how to build; continual overtaking of the processes of construction is what we mean by knowledge. To discover like points is the function of primary intuition; as a result of this act differences are secondarily disclosed. Uniformity is what we should seek. The condition of association is the condition of good management. Social law is the economic law. When economic utilities were made with tools, opportunities were freer and the laborer had a chance to breathe; he was then upon the general public directly dependent, and for him there was social hope, that is, were he from godly control of kings and vicegerents indemnified by being in a country akin to what ours was for a time after the Revolution.

Wasn't *that* a glorious strike against tyranny? Stirred by an overmastering sense of the sacredness of their natural rights, stung into perception of their duty to the individual self, our people with dignity rose up, united; the men and women became strikers, would no longer brook "oppression's heel." Read their Declaration of Independence, and its grand soul you will feel. In the army and navy was the tyrant's hope. Our people stood united. God be thanked for strikes and strikers!

At the patience of the poor I marvel. By the vast use of vast machinery production is effected. Division of labor is multiform and varied. Our socio-industrial methods may be likened to the sun, upon whose rays, for a chance to live, each being is directly dependent. Now let us assume the doings of that mighty orb de-communized, brought under the individual control of our coal barons, they who produce an artificial scarcity of fuel, who fill their pockets by freezing their fellows, freezing some of them to death. But then our country's manufacturers must be protected, and against the dangers of a comfortable fire the laborer secured by a representative government. Association is not the condition of good management, and the social law is not the economic law. Do away with the use of machinery, return to individual methods of production? What absurdity! I trust I hear the evolution-sound better. There is a pig to be roasted; to accomplish the feat I leave to men the practical logic of burning the house down. Onward, ever onward, is my motto; give loose rein unto the intellect; more machinery and better, fine and finer work; but that which is unnatural (individual control) I would wipe out.

Imagine the two halves of a sphere out of relation, not adjusted to each other. Economics is a sphere. Production implies distribution. The methods of production are co-operative, are socialistic. The state of distribution is anarchistic. Are beauty and the beast a well-matched pair? Increased use of machinery marks the evolution of the race. By individual control the greatest blessing is converted into a social Juggernaut, into a curse. "O foolish men, what hath bewitched you" that ye see not the simplest truths of relation? The two halves of a sphere must be mated, their positions must match.

That which is unnatural is pre-doomed. On track of consistency our men are not keen-scented hounds. By the money mirage and the word "earn" do not longer be befooled; open your eyes and look beneath the surface; it will do you good to strain your intellectual vision; remember there's reward; the senses came through tensive effort. Economic utilities should, by the laws of motion, by reaction, move backward to their source, to the laborer. Possession by appropriation has quite another source. With constructive labor be pleased to correlate the motions of the entrepreneur. Profits unsocialized, it is to the money interest of the controller of production to make things scarce and dear. The principle of capitalistic production is, the least possible supply to the consumer consistent with the greatest possible gain to myself; accordingly social anomalies. Machines are in existence that, were they operated in the interest of all, would relieve everyone from drudgery, and would make nobody one whit the worse off; and yet for general use such machines are inaccessible, are in fact converted by the few into a means by which they cudgel the many.

I have seen machines which ironed hundreds of shirts in a day, and yet their feet were not tired, and their backs did not ache. Now, think of women perspiring over flatirons. Bah! the thing is sickening. Why, so easy is it to produce, that capitalism, if left to itself, would fade away into the dim and misty space of nowhere; but bolstered up by vicious under-legislation it stays with us, assists in the intellectual and moral progress of society. Capitalism, "red in tooth and claw," violates the sanctity of home life, drags wives and mothers to its foul embrace. Unsatisfied, it stops not; there are the children; aye, the monster would clutch from the cradle unweaned babes could their tiny fingers hold a bobbin. How men do respect the home and the women when they have a lust to be gratified! An economic philanthropist, a millionaire, briefly precipitated capitalism's whole matter when he said, "The public be damned."

Knowing something of the facts of motion and of the facts of form, I know where to relation actions that are stamped illegal, such as counterfeiting, stealing, and burglary. Never do I look at a prison *home (?)*, never do I think of one, but my soul is filled with horror for the iniquity, not of those who are inside. Every impure thought, every grasping desire, finds a lodgment somewhere in that picture-gallery, the mind. Political society is not a pattern housekeeper, he is not clean ; conditions are filthy and breed moral vermin. Is there prostitution ? Why, then it comes in answer to the demand of our men. While women by conditions are made economically dependent, some of them have no choice, no other means by which to get a living. Economic communism, socialism, would indeed be a disastrous thing, would interfere with male legislation on the "age of consent." As long as the ballot expresses brutal feelings and does not represent ideas, society will have a moral stench. Men, unlike the vestal virgins, prepare themselves for the sacrifice by no purifying rites.

Now, is it not just a trifle officious in authority to tell us that men are in the image of their Maker? Watch their conduct ; a holy exhibit, isn't it? While society is political, while there is violation of the moral law, illegal acts are merely responses to the political liturgy; but when an atrocity is committed the difference to the offender is great, is dependent upon which side of the fence he was on at the time he dealt morality the blow. Our other selves, illegal offenders against the moral law, "with the justice of your cause few are concerned."

In the West a star has arisen; there an administrator avers that in the case of an employee's dereliction, it is just and it is wise to take into consideration the example set him by the employing corporation. God be thanked for Altgeld, governor of Illinois. This attitude saves from pure rottenness the administration of our socio-industrial Sodom and Gomorrah.

Motions, according to their character, are classified into constructive and destructive. To plant your field with wheat, stumps must be removed; could the stumps speak they would say — anarchist. The operations of the mind reveal that builder and anarchist travel together; evolution, holding the rein, guides; philosophic anarchism accompanies reason's work, but is reason chained, then anarchism has no choice, has to work by its other method.

A mind gives to the world its ideas; is that mind's enjoyment of its own thereby lessened? Not a whit; its enjoyment is enhanced by sharing.

Myself with others; communism is the socio-psychological rule and to it there is no exception. Blundering Om. Look, that idea takes on gross material form, and among the means of production it is placed. And now note the character of the procedure: myself *with* others is the exception; myself *against* others, myself *without* others, is invariably the rule. Men are loth to break, by an occasional godlike blunder, the monotony of perfection that attends their socio-industrial work. To vary uniformity is sometimes well; their case would by such complication seem, at least to me, more hopeful.

Man's practical reasoning says, I am no marauder; look, I have gewgaws, am stamped, am, you see, under orders; mine is the holy crusade, legal indulgence to murder folks outright, or, stopping short of that, to produce at least a lingering death by robbing them of their opportunities. Still I am human; who can challenge the fact? Is not such absurdity, I ask, enough to convulse the very fiends in hell with uproarious laughter? Heaven was not reached by that tower in Babel; yet listen to the verdict of our men. Competition is great, is our motor impulse; through its operations all socio-industrial progress is made. Improvements in machinery are wrought, and a cheapening of fabrics is the result of competition; discoveries have been made because of it. Competition produces wealth, gives us cheap oil. And the Standard Oil Company? I queried. Well, not exactly; consolidation, union, was the cause of that. There are occasions when competition is in abeyance and goes to the wall. Still, you will allow that competition is just wonderful; to the delectation of its plutocratic rider it heads in opposite directions at the same time. I reckon that you are without the experiences furnished by our gas companies; why, if it were not for competition they'd eat us up, leave nothing for food and clothes and our poor landlords. At all events, from time to time the city council by logic is convinced, new franchises are bestowed, streets torn up, and dirt, dirt. No matter; that makes work, and work is the thing we want.

Now, did women manage their domestic affairs on the political plan, where, oh where, would society land? Happily they don't, their imitation of the politico-economic ways of men goes no further than the production of crazy quilts. But then women are not creators, are limited to fancy.

The men exercise imagination, and while I don't deny that in their doings they always have in view an objective end, still at all times the all-important business on *their* hands is to create an appearance, a bustle. In medicine persistent confusion is attributed to vertigo, to lightness of the head. What competition does is to loosen the grasp of an individual appropriation. Competition produces nothing; why, how can it? Yet the men don't see it. I wonder are they arrant liars, or is theirs a case of uncomplicated ———

And now, my sisters, a word to you. Be not disturbed, nor by trifles overwrought. Should I say the sun shone not, would the fact be altered by a say-so? About that challenge of our title to "curves," lines of beauty, what did it matter? There is, however, one undoubted fact: no chance for a contest over which sex has the corner on curves in the mind, corner on curves in the morals. Again, I urge, be not officious; Mother Nature needeth not your help, she is equal to the work, has all eternity in which to do a stupendous job, endow our Schopenhauers with brains.

Socialism (I will trouble you to consult a a dictionary) — socialism, like woman, has a character, and at present, unlike woman's, it is bad. The cause, germs in the thought-atmosphere, and of course heredity. To discover the origin of these germs we must travel backward to our long-past ancestry. By the bull's fierce ravings the herd deemed itself protected; did not know that those ravings really invited battle. The international thought had not taken root; doings were prompted, not by the social feeling, but by the political thought. Such is the origin of the paternal or political socialism which among humans is extant.

One must go deeper for the cause of its perpetuation. As we have seen, the male was biologically started on an everlasting tour, with his actual possessions in the form of potentialities; by experience of what is in the external he has built up solidity. Still he moves forward only as he is moved by hard knocks. Man sees things on the bias, does not see them on the straight; consequently we have paternal or political socialism.

I am asked my opinion of Henry Wood and his book. Here it is; take it. I feel pity for the urchin who fumbles in the gutter, who collects and piles up the stumps of dirty cigars, but his vocation — ugh! — I despise. When I read upon the title page of a book, "The Political Economy of Natural Law," words which, if they mean anything, mean the party management of natural conditions, and then observe how widely separated are the contents of said book and its title, I want to be a sister to that author, advise him for his good, advise him to get a pocket dictionary. But then to the business world Henry Wood claims that his books are acceptable. Need more be said?

"Wealth and Progress," by George Gunton. Build up the wants of the poor? Ah! somewhere I have seen it stated that an eminent lawyer, when summing up his case in few but fitting words, briefly disposed of a witness whose perjury was made apparent by frantic efforts to debauch the jury-mind: And I now come, gentlemen of the jury, to the testimony of John Van Zandt, may God have mercy on his soul. "Peace, peace, and there is no peace."

Professor Bemis, with an eye half open, utters a mild protest against the violent infraction of moral law and order by trusts and monopolies, but he is not for this thrown out of the Chicago

University; a subsidized institution does not act in that way. It is not an anarchist. *This is how it does it.* Note the difference in method, and note the difference to Prof. Bemis in the resulting end. The president, Christ's apostle upon the earth, a representative of His, gives the sinner warning that criticizing money-mongers is unchrist-like and objectionable to "my lord;" then, merely as a matter of emphasis, to objectivize the disapprobation of wrongdoing, the president, either in a direct or a roundabout way, calls for Prof. B's *voluntary* resignation, which despite an alternative is tendered. That is all there is to it. Now, are you the person, in the face of purifying ceremonies, forms, to persist in misplacing the word anarchist? Chicago's capitalistic waters were troubled, were roiled, but oil was at hand. Uprose the sleek, smooth Harper, his lamp was full and trimmed, himself was ready to obey the behests of KING MONEY. Lumped, his actions and his words amount to just this: By the facts of structure, by the modes of motion, zoölogists may classify the animals with which they deal ; that such is the scientific method of arrangement I don't deny, but I follow no such stupid example, am not bound down, hampered, by principles of law and order. For an anarchist am I to be mistaken? My education in the arts has been better. Trust me, I, the Lord's anointed, hear the still small voice and know how to treat my master brute.

Natural selection has produced a variety of socio-economic talkers, whose differences are found in their pin feathers and not in their plumage, and so Professor Laughlin protests that there is no such thing as a labor problem ; the whole matter in sum and substance amounts to simply this : idleness, viciousness, crime. True, professor dear, but art sure that you are equal to locating that category? Cornell mourns, has lost a professorial curiosity, one whose powers of logical thought are not entirely " out of sight," not beyond the reach of woodchuck and of mole. Prof. Laughlin is an explorer, is of an inductive turn of mind, has a discovery made, unearthed a brilliant : what the plutocrat receives is merely wages for his skill in managing. Management of what? Management for what? Why so chary of thy knowledge? "Marry, sirrah, I'd have thee beaten" for KING MONEY'S jester.

Strange, is it not, that folks persist in confusing labor with laborer, capital with capitalist, and cap the climax by using interchangeably the terms laborer and commodity, the thing the laborer produces. Among educated persons there exists a lamentable want of penetration into the contents of words; it is shown even by Mr. Stead, he who is distressed lest, slighting good London, Christ should come to wicked Chicago. Unacquainted with Chicago's coterie of earnest socialistic women, he is hard upon the windy city. Even he does not know the meaning and the application of the little word "expose."

One portion of the variety of talkers to which I have referred avers that things are really wrong and do need straightening, that economic changes of necessity must come, and then there will be a marked, a great improvement. They protest, however, that we are not ready for improvement; to straighten is positively dangerous; might snap the social spine, might break society's broad back. These who so affirm are our vindicated, timid, our loving little fearful Elyites.

You are hungry; the hour is noon; by hunger nature gets you ready for a reception, dinner. When it is due, the laborer wants his week's pay; a demagogue strives through legislation to secure the workingman this great favor. The affrighted banker shrieks "over-legislation." Queer, isn't it?

A book is in my hand, its title "Justice;" a misnomer. Its author, indeed I am ashamed to tell it, is Herbert Spencer, he who wrote "First Principles." "How are the mighty fallen!" The mountain which on high ejected substance, fire and lava, now belches forth just dirty smoke, bedraggled ideas. "Can a man enter his mother's womb and be born again?" I should say it would at least be well to take a fresh start.

In other days it was the custom to entertain,

to amuse, by the method of telling stories. For the *dramatis personæ* is my audience ready? I must advise, however, that, taken together, their strains prove no symphony, pitched to different keys as you will at once perceive; yet from the overtones each one of you may gather the music of knowledge. The one first upon my list is no stranger; the principles he embodies are in fact the co-respondent to our almost every thought. Principle of sympathy is not, as you know, in our social drama, cast to an intelligent part.

Mr. Individualist: "Ladies and gentlemen, I shall not occupy at length your valuable time, nor do I apprehend that upon this occasion it is necessary. I advocate principles which have not to build up new mental states, nor make additions to the soul. I am not a socialist. Always has it been my luck to find a chord vibrating responsive to my touch. I wish this morning to call attention to the characteristic greatness of the age in which we live, surrounded as we are by the works of art and artizan; and permit me to arrest for a few brief moments the diffusiveness of your thought, by nailing it to a point — the reason of our greatness. To what do we owe advancement — the distance between us and savages? I expect the soulful response, amen, to come from every person present when I shall have named the grand cause — individual freedom and competition. To shackle the limbs of man is a tyrant's work, and he who does it is the violator of the 'formula of justice;' every man is free to do that which he wills, provided he infringes not the equal freedom of any other man.

"But, my friends, though man has a right to unshackled limbs, and a right to physical integrity, and though of some of the 'natural media' he has the right of use, yet Almighty wisdom has seen fit through man, His image, to draw the line upon equal individual freedom, and to arrest it at the land point. The principle of inequality must by my lambs be maintained, saith the Lord. The inconceivable advantages accruing from this arrest have, by 'a distinguished thinker,' the Rev. T. R. Malthus, been exposed;

his keen intellect probed this matter to the very core. Accordingly we know that by land monopoly wealth has been spontaneously created; by this device nature, mean, niggardly mother nature, is compelled to give her destitute children a bounty — rent.

"Nor is this benefit all; the great science has discovered that increase in the amount of cultivation is in direct ratio to decrease in the number of persons having an opportunity to work the land. Man, ladies and gentlemen, is a many-sided being, but when considering him in an industrial aspect, disturbing elements must be eliminated. With the economic conception simplified, man, ladies and gentlemen, stands forth a creature moved by but a single impulse, gain; actuated by but one desire, greed. Over mountain steeps, through gorges and ravines, he climbs, he wades, he dives, for *his own* gain. Shall we hamper the heroic spirit? *Laissez faire* is the word. I ask, is society equal to the 'conception of a harmonious life,' equal to the establishment of conditions calculated to call out the better side of man's nature? Suppose the ridiculous proposition is admitted, then I ask, have you the conscience to encourage sin, over-legislation, interference with individual freedom, change the conception of what is required in economic man? To public schools I say, get thee behind me, Satan; myself would put them down by the law's strong arm. In that Utopia, 'Looking Backward', socio-economic equality is pictured, everybody is put on a level. The thing is unnatural; *brains* must tell; can't bring a millionaire down to the position of a pauper. Shouldn't a man have what he earns?"

(Voice from the audience: "Which man?")

"To assume that men either can or will live harmoniously in the socio-economic state, myself with others their inspiring thought, is, to say the least, trifling, and to assume that competition can be tamely directed along the line of equal effort to do honest, good work, is, ladies and gentlemen, in my humble opinion an agitating thought, is in short an anarchistic move, and I am not an anarchist."

(Voice : "Then you disapprove of the American Revolution?")

"By the principles and methods advocated in the Utopia to which I have referred, 'the intellectually and physically feeble are to be quite as well off as others.' Now, I have a question to ask of this intelligent audience, which will, I think, settle this whole matter right here and for all time : Which of you would like to have your poor old father, your aged, decrepit mother, an invalid sister, or, it may be, a feeble-minded brother, economically independent, provided with all comforts, conditions which are desired by your own strong self? Why, the thing is anarchistic, economically impious, denies the principle of inequality, exalts the principle of intelligent sympathy; it ought not, cannot, shall not be. See 'formula of justice.' Competition, ladies and gentlemen, is so closely connected with freedom that one can scarcely say which is Minerva and which is Jove. Amidst the buffetings which on every hand beset individual freedom, let us offer a pæan of praise, for competition is free. Hallelujah!"

Before introducing the next speaker, as presiding officer of this meeting I wish to say that the desire is to preserve as large an amount of individual freedom as is consistent with social decorum, therefore questions and remarks are in order after the speaker has sat down. Will Mr. Individualist show us how his use of the generic term, man, how his general explanation of man's nature, either accounts for or justifies the socio-economic atrocity of society's division into those who *produce* and those who *pillage the producer?* I confess that I for one do not perceive the point of application.

"Really, madam, the point which you have raised requires hours for its elucidation; there are other speakers, and time is pressing; pray excuse me if I decline to attempt important matter requiring more time than, at present, is at our disposal."

The chair asks the favor of making a few remarks. From the expressions of our honored speaker I have inferred that he deems fraternal socialism a state unnatural to people, to us humans. Sir, is my inference right, or do I stand corrected? Is it not a fact that things, according to the position they occupy in time and space, are either natural or unnatural? If this be so, does the principle which determines naturalness or unnaturalness cease to work as we cease to deal with the apparently objective things of time and space? I think not; its application to the phenomena in Beings-space, in Species-time, is no less valid. And again I ask, is it not a fact, that of living beings each species has its peculiar, its differentiating principle, which informs and animates its social motions, and that conduct, to be natural to a species, must be dictated by, and in line with, that species' informing principle? Things are right and natural only when particulars fit into generals. Upon the fact of progress I think we all agree. Now, if the human principle in its general social workings is so little different from that which animates the herbivora, why, I, for one, propose that we throw off hypocrisy, do the creditable—go upon all fours.

Guided by the "legal merits of the case" society tolerates invasion of equal, of natural, rights to opportunities, tolerates moral lawlessness.

He who is next upon my list is the product of the capitalistic régime, political or paternal socialism. Ladies and gentlemen, I now introduce the Tramp; upon him observe the nævus-paternus.

Tramp: "Tell my story? It's not uncommon; 'millions in it.' Well, when I was young we kept our heads above water, had comforts, though father was inclined to drink. Vested interests must be supported; they are the important thing, are after profits, and so the liquor poison is itself poisoned. Father died. I, the eldest born, was fifteen, hated liquor, would not drink, left school, and went to work. The family should be kept from sinking into deeper poverty, and out working my mother should never go; so I planned and so I hoped. Forget that morning, the one when I, a child, put my shoulder to the wheel, started life as a man, went out, sought work? No, by Joe! With joy my heart beat high. Glad and proud was I to feel myself a great, strong boy. You see, it never entered my head that opportunities wouldn't meet me half way. Oh! the disappointment and the shame. Yes, I got the job and I got the pay, $1.50 for a whole week's work. My boss wasn't that Fall River overseer who boasts of pulling his company out of insolvency by fining and docking its employees, but still you can bet he was no angel. Weren't the Christian Fathers too saving of their good capital when they allowed there was only one devil? There are legions; wherever there is a chance to boss, they swarm. Why, every hospital, every public home, throughout this or any other land, has its tyrants, has its petty czars. You see, I have been in some of them, have had experiences. Have been arrested for vagrancy too; but without a home to go to, what does one expect a cove to do? I can't live on thin air, and from off the earth I can't take my feet. My spirit is willing sometimes but pretty generally the flesh is weak. God Almighty didn't intend the stomach to be filled with air, meant that for the lungs; and from the signs I reckon that He's gitting things ready for a startling revelation of His will about feet and the earth.

"I was a steady boy and stayed years in my first place. I liked machinery, used to think I heard it talk. All the time my mind was running on invention; at last I did turn out an improvement; that's the time I was happy. But, say, folks, do I look like as if by using my brains I had been benefited any? And yet they say brains tell. Now, I've got a sense of humor, and miserable as I am, I couldn't keep from laughing over Mr. Individualist's talk. Them kind of lies don't bother me now, but they used to. You see, ladies and gentlemen, the last few years I have been a tourist, a gentleman of leisure; been too old to compete with the younger brood. You see, God failed to provide for this emergency, and so I have been thinking, and I have been reasoning quite a good deal, and upon more things than one; sometimes have been almost happy, not because of my wretched affairs, but in spite of 'em.

"But now about these Mr. Individualists: well, I conclude it's a pity Balaam's ass started perpetual motion, left these fellows without time to think. A different state of affairs would interfere with individual freedom, would it? Rob inventors of their lawful gains, damp the heroic spirit? Holy Moses! to make things worse, at least for some of us, a different state of affairs would have to climb something more substantial than a Jacob's ladder. I haven't lived fifty years, haven't been knocked around from pillar to post, for nothing; I've got my eyes open, had 'em open from first to last; just had to, or would have been wiped off the earth. The law of self-preservation with the tramp is uppermost, exactly as it is with you folks, and don't you forget it. I could tell you this morning of present doings, and of doings to come. With a warning the very air is heavy, Don't you feel it?

Naw, you don't; if you did, souls that are 'way down out of sight would creep up and through, would show on the outside, and then the clouds would be lifted, drift away, away, leave things bright and sunshiny, not for you alone, but for me too. But, pshaw! it's no use to talk; I don't stand here for to herald a Johnstown flood; sleep on; the poor old tramp may help, but he cannot hinder the inevitable.

"While economic conditions are such that the devil operates men, society wouldn't be better off could food be created up in the air; when it floated to the earth 'twould all be cornered, and some of us would still be homeless tramps. 'The foxes have holes, and the birds of the air have nests,' but the son of the capitalistic system has not where to lay his head. The burning question of the hour is not the labor problem, but it is, What *don't* our plutocrats want?

"Where was I in my story? Guess I've rambled, the habit of the tramp;—let me see: oh, yes, my invention. I couldn't take out a patent, had no money. Company offered me a royalty. I agreed. Typhoid fever took me; plumbing in our dwelling bad: we were poor folks; see? The corporation allowed me half pay; at the time I thought that was just too good, have seen through it since. When I was getting well—convalescing, the doctor called it—the overseer came, said they had about concluded my invention wasn't worth a patent, still, as they had used it, and at the same time had great sympathy for me, they had thought the matter over, and had decided that, if I would sign away my rights, they would give me one hundred dollars. The overseer said I should be grateful for this, look upon it as an out and out present. It went agin the grain, but mother was tired, needed rest, couldn't just then go out to day's work; so I succumbed; besides, my situation was at stake if I refused. It seems to me that one, has he a pennyweight of brains, must allow that things are wrong when a willing man has to beg of his fellow-men a chance to work. Things are wrong when revenge, because an imposition is resented, when personal pique throws a poor man out of a chance to get a living, steals his opportunity to express his human powers.

"Now, I could understand these things were some men monsters like them mammoths I have seen in picture books. To live, to get a chance to work, some men must play the sycophant, must cringe; I wasn't built that way, if I *am* poor. To steal, I sometimes think, is just as honorable and more consistent with a body's sense of dignity. Why, by stealing, the tramp may get a shelter in some prison home, but by cringing — *ugh!* And this is the alternative society forces upon its most impoverished folks. Heigh-ho! what it is to feel your hand against everyone, and everyone's hand against you. But I didn't begin it, though. The shoe that society throws after me has a leg in it. Whew! I, a nobody, am moralizing. Now, don't I know a tramp's thoughts and feelings is not counted in? He is lazy, because he don't like the work you, my good gentlemen or lady, thinks fit to set him. Awful, ain't it?

"And so individual freedom would be wrecked were the industrial plant run in the interest of everybody, were the people mutually equally dependent, mutually equally independent of each other? But then wouldn't this gripless tourist be out of his present lucrative job? Why, I feel demoralized by the very thought. I've a venturesome spirit, though, and would like to try that kind of socialism. And now I come to think on it, with a square chance possibly I might come out natural, might come straight up, like a bird whose clipped wings have at last a longed-for chance to grow. As I look around upon nature, it strikes me God's ways of working is to keep things that are alike together; guess that's why He started the human race as a family. But it's me that's found man's way of doing business is to scatter; wonder who is man's prompter.

"Ladies and gentlemen, that corporation changed its mind about my invention; using it yet. Health returned and with it hope. I was young, twenty-four, determined not to be beat down, but to invent something more, and this time *I* was to be the one who should reap; at least that is the way I settled it. But, by gracious! they got the best of me again, this time by taking the matter into court. It was a technical point on which I was worsted; at least that's what the wranglers said. I s'pose they thought I was comforted, but that's the time I shut down shop, hated folks, discouraged, took sick, brain fever. Wouldn't go back to the factory; afraid I'd kill somebody.

"Now, when I started life I was happy, towards everybody felt friendly; what think you brought about the change? Too much 'free will,' maybe; but it wasn't mine. Yes, I've gone to the bad, but then I'm not badly scared; reckon an impartial Judge, one not bought up with corporation money, one not influenced by the thought of votes, will know about how far to hold a fellow responsible for his feelings and his acts when things outside of him are goading, just eating right into his flesh and bone. And I want right here to tell you, folks, that I've had a blamed

hard fight with conditions, and you'll allow that
I've had nothing whatever to do with the making
of our industrial arrangements. Say, look here,
am I represented in Congress? And yet they
call this a free country. One thing is certain,
the poor in this callithumpian republic are free
to be robbed of their rights, and are free to
starve. I'm let beautifully into this open secret.

"When I got up from the brain fever I took
a position on the street cars, was conductor,
worked seventeen hours per diem. Oh, no, that
wasn't regular pay time. You see, the company
is smart, contrives to rub extras in on a fellow.
Now don't you fall into an error and think the
men who do the work are the ones to be benefited. I allow, that would be the natural thing,
but society ain't built that way; the harvest of
gain is reaped by figureheads. You can just
bet that the denomination on the workingman's
note shows up mighty small; it's the loafers,
them's the fellers that draws the great pay.
Doing night work my fingers and toes froze, and
I lost my right foot, was in the hospital, laid up

for months. That was the last straw. Poor mother took sick, lost heart, died; and I, and I, maybe I wasn't desperate, took to drink, didn't care if I went to the bad. Hadn't I been willing to work? And to think the children were scattered, were out of school, were in the factory.

"Before things got so bad I was ambitious to be somebody, read a good deal, wanted to keep up with the times, be posted on things in general; used to buy newspapers; some of them are more than half on the side of the working people. And then, too, I belonged to a club, went to lectures. Why, once some university professors was invited to address us on protection and economics. Protection, ha! ha! that subject I gave the 'go-by' to. Why, a man with a spark of mother-wit sees its meaning; plutocratic, plutocratic through and through. But I wanted to know something of economics, so I went to hear that professor. Jiminy! them's the fellers, regular agitators, the worst in the market. Why, I just had to hold on to my coat-collar to keep from jumping at that one's throat. You see, his fool talk maddened me and I wanted to choke it off. Why, if you'll believe it, that blasted idiot stood up before us workin' people and said the reason why so many men were out of employment was because they wasn't skilful, didn't do good work. The capitalists, he said, weren't to blame; they couldn't help it, Now, for a cheerful liar, what do you think of that? My fingers just itched to wring his neck. I'd like to know when *I* refused a suit of broadcloth clothes just because they weren't of the finest quality. Just now my wardrobe needs repairing and additions. Suppose some of you try an experiment and find out for yourselves how near that university feller hit the mark. Come, I'd like to help you find the truth in this matter. His talk on demand and supply was a sickener too, was the sheerest tomfoolery; he said that, to raise the price of a commodity, to make a thing dear, shut off the demand; folks didn't want it then. And if I don't disremember, it was somewhere here that he wrung the word 'effective' in, and by the use of that particler word he allowed he'd just got things down fine; had got production and distribution adjusted, relationed, as he called it. I want to be charitable to my feller-creeters that are not overstocked, be as kind as some of the Red Indians that I have read about. If that professor lacked gumption— Still, I don't know about *that*.

"All the time he was talking to us men he did so put me in mind of a reciter I once saw at the time that man was doing Uriah Heap—one of Dickens' characters, you know. Dickens was a great writer, wasn't he? His books did lots of good. After all, I believe that professor from the University of Penn was up to devilish tricks. We workingmen could have let him into a thing or two; his pizen got no chance to work in *our* minds. You see, labor, honest fulfilment of the divine decree, lets men into truth. Talking lies is a vested interest, just as much as selling liquor; both of 'em are direct taxes on an individual. The one aims direct for the brain, the other direct for the soul.

"Now, don't I want a house, want a home, instead of traipsing the streets nights? Thank goodness, my turn at the Salvation Army's home has come; I sleep there to-night. Them's good folks and Christians too, as far as they can get a chance to go. Walking the streets cold nights I stand and look at the churches, and I wonder why the doors don't fly open; seems as if they must, and let me inside, let me from the wind and rain be sheltered. Why, by mere device the Saviour is denied, by bolts and bars is hindered from succoring a forlorn and helpless creature, ME. Why, to be happy one must have his wants supplied HERE and in the hereafter too, must have comforts. In the eyes of the All-wise can the future be more important than the NOW? Why, how *can* it be? I conclude something's wrong; our religious affairs are out of gear. Had I been among the first to dig beneath the crust, make this discovery, I calkilate I wouldn't be left to freeze, neither would I have been consulted about the amount of fire necessary to my comfort. The pious were awfully attentive to the helpless, had special preparation for the work. Prompted by the Christian spirit, the *burning* question was their particular forte. Inside God's house on Sundays there's no end of talk, real 'soft sodder'; why, some men are trained to it and earn their living in that way. Maybe it's honest, and maybe it ain't; at any rate, it don't make things better, don't help the tramp's cause.

"What's the good of preachers anyway? 'Taint apparent to me. They're pretty generally on the wrong side. They were for the slaveowner down South; worked with all their might and main to keep the colored folks from thinkin', and actin'. You allow 'twas dreadful for the chosen of the Lord to labor hard just to keep those poor black creeturs down. They fulfilled divine decree; they earned their bread by the sweat of their brow, didn't they? Why, they actilly desecrated the Lord's day, broke the Sabbath by preachin' that slavery was right and pious, that it was lawful to hold a colored brother, and as like as not one's own black child, as personal property, and claimed to prove it by the Bible. When there's an injustice, an iniquity, to be sustained, don't it really seem that gospel ministers, accootred with the Bible, are right on hand anxious for the job? And, by Jingo! their's is the magical work, the wonderfullest tricks you ever saw; got the bulge on God's laws, and to the cross-eyed soul religious experts make black look white. Look this matter up for yourselves; go in deep, don't skim the surface; see if you don't find that, as a class, ministers of the gospel are as a rule agin the oppressed and on the side of the oppressor; are afraid of the grand bounce, I suppose; leastways, it appears mainly to be a matter of filthy lucre, and not mainly a matter of following AN EXAMPLE.

"Whew! I must stop this; thinkin' on so much wickedness is demoralizing to a feller; I'll shift my thoughts to something better,

"But, see here: don't you make a mistake and accuse this poor old tramp of not believing in futurity existence, in the hereafter. Why, haven't I listened to the voice of machinery, haven't I looked upon the heavens, felt the starry whispers? This tramp *knows* there is everlasting life, gets his knowledge of it from the 'Source.' For truth I don't go to poll-parrots. All I want in this world is a chance to get my living without offering up prayers to any partic'lar person, or giving special thanks for the favor; I want a meal of victuals, and I don't want to saw a cord of wood—sawin' wood ain't my forte—and so when I can I get the victuals, and then I skip. Shocked, are you, my benefactor? S'pose you put your thinkin' cap on and see if two hasn't a right to play at the game of gouge. Fringe upon society, are tramps? Now, are they? Look here, how does it happen that fringe adorns a shawl? Don't know? Well, I'll help you out of the quandary; part of the shawl has been ravelled out, that's all; see? When I was a little feller I had a playmate who would step on my toes, kept right on after I had asked him not to and told him that it hurt; that made me mad, and I thought, My mister, I'll fix you;

so to get square I stamped back. I allow 'twasn't right, but all the same 'twas natural and acted like a charm.

"If the labor unions took up our cause, but they don't; seems as if they ought to have a fellow-feelin' for us, give us hope and not the cold shoulder. Society stamps on me, makes me feel as if I were a fiend from hell, shoves me out a tramp. Say, good folks, when at night you shut your doors, seek your bed and blankets, do you ever think of the homeless ones? Consoled, aren't you, by the thought, 'Well, they're a bad lot'? Guess you never done a sum in vulgar fractions, or you'd 'a' seen cancellation's work. Why, the figures above the line, them that's on top, just 'knock the spots' out of the feller underneath.

Think fur 'nuff, make a social application, find out how it stands between the individooal acts of the upper and the lower classes. S'pose you put your intellects to work, imagine what it is never to be sure of a bed, sure of a good square meal, what it is to be always certain of cold and hunger. Humor this tramp's whim just for fun, and then examine your feelin's, take account of the stock you have on hand. I'm thinkin' you'll be smitten with knowledge, and I'm bettin' right here that if some of you go over your tea or tobacco time there's no livin' with you. *Your* feelin's are on parade; that's all right; but when *my* feelin's make the show the case is different. Dissected, wouldn't it turn out that tramps have nerves, that tramps have hearts no furder in than yours? Placed in our conditions, no comforts and no HOME, wouldn't you feel desperate, and, feeling desperate, wouldn't you act so? God Almighty made us men; social conditions made us tramps, and don't you forget it. Jumped on from every quarter, given at useful steady work not the ghost of a chance, wont somebody get right up and tell me what a man is to do with his strength and his courage? 'Brains tell.' I will put mine to work; I'll go to counterfeiting, help disturb the circulation, aid the bankers. Mr. Individualist says I've a right to voluntary motion; so don't you interfere. Adieu; I am off, and I am onto society."

With a mirthless laugh he went; and Greek meets Greek. Friends, judge in yourselves, is it seemly for a man to be a multi-millionaire?

I must ask the audience, would they hear the baby's wail, to keep very quiet. Accustomed to the sounds, with your permission I will them interpret. "I am cold and hungry, have no warm clothes, am barefoot, winter and no fire; want my mamma, she's out washing, begged me to be good and quiet, tied up in this chair; said she'd bring me food; can't wait, I'm hungry." But, baby, see; thy little toes should have dug a way up Lord Gorilla's back, then thou would'st not be in want; born without the money-caul, civilized society has in thee no vested interest, owes thee nothing. Why amongst us Christians did'st thou come? Thou should'st have gone unto those savages whose system of exchange is unnatural, "they who make presents to each other;" there, baby dear, thy social lot had been different; we are Christians, and out of each other must make profits. The Chinese father counts his babes redundant, puts them in conditions where he knows that they will perish, sees they die. Parental monster! Christian society's political father manages, it is true, somewhat differently. *His* redundant babes perish in conditions himself hath made ; still the political father is well bred, is gentlemanly, turns aside, does not watch them die. Christian civilized society is bigger than a Chinese father ; ought it not to have a bigger human heart ?

> " Not more than others I deserve, yet God hath given me more,
> For I have food while others starve, and beg from door to door."

The gentleman and lady whom I now present to you are engaged in charitable work. Ladies and gentlemen, the Reverend Mr. Underdone and Miss Seethroughit.

Rev. Mr. Underdone (speaking drawingly) : " Friends, it is with a feeling of humility that I open my lips this morning. Having for years labored in the charitable field, I am by experience able to testify that, instead of the poor being elevated by my efforts, they are sinking deeper into poverty; their numbers increase with alarming rapidity. I am baffled, am humbled in the sight of the Lord. Deep dejection fills my soul, ladies and gentlemen. Food and clothes are perishable, and the poor *will* eat. Feed them, and they don't *stay* fed; in a few hours they are again clamoring for food. Then, too, their clothes wear out, and walking is hard upon their shoes. Oh! oh! [sighs] I have, ladies and gentlemen, about concluded that it is useless to do anything for the poor. Woe is me, the way is dark; and yet a glimmer of light I see in the hope of a discovery how to keep the poor from getting hungry, how to walk and not wear out their shoes. In the meantime it might be well if good, charitable persons would go down to the poor and teach them how to help themselves; their case would be hopeful if they could be gotten to imitate the example of our millionaires, gotten to practice the virtue of abstinence, self-denial. Lacking the divine spark, they are obdurate. I am, ladies and gentlemen, on my way this morning to consult Mr. Moneybags, a pillar in my church, on the expediency of appointing an hour of prayer to lay my suggestions before the Lord."

Miss Seethroughit (speaking earnestly): "I went to the college settlement with the intention of teaching the poor how to be economical and saving, knowledge which at that time I thought they lacked. My eyes are opened. I have concluded that to intrude upon them is impertinence. It is we, the would-be instructors, who have learned useful lessons. A great social wrong exists when conditions cause the extremes of luxury and poverty. I see the rich getting richer, and the poor getting poorer, and I unhesitatingly affirm that the education needed by the poor is that which helps them to come into a knowledge of their social rights, that which helps them to the knowledge that they have a right to exercise their human powers. Things cannot go on in this way much longer; familiarity with the principles of chemistry leads me to declare that the final result of such combination is social explosion" (speaking very earnestly). "Since leaving the college settlement I have been occupied with that class of persons whom society is pleased to call fallen women, and, ladies and gentlemen, you may believe me when I tell you, that my ideas on this social matter have undergone regeneration, have in fact been born anew. With the whole subject I am so full of thought that were I this morning to open the floodgates of my soul, 'twould drown you out. The difference between fallen men and women is superficial, is a matter of social position, a matter of mere appearance. Reality lies deeper; of the two, fallen women have more of the human, and I want this morning to propose that we women found a home for fallen men, the management of which should be philosophic, should be high art. To call up a realization of the beauty of the good, every effort must be tried. My! if we could only make their entrance into it compulsory, lots of families would, I know, be robbed of their male members;

but then the compensation! They would get their men folks back changed in thought; think of *that.*"

Indeed I am nonplussed, I hardly know by what cognomen to introduce the personage next upon my list; nomenclature fails me. Ah! for that timely suggestion I thank you.

Society's Quack Doctor: "Here you are, ladies and gentlemen, walk right up, secure a recipe; don't be backward; a large assortment, all first class, that I offer, all alive and kicking; warranted to cure the ailments of society; warranted to chase a monstrous brood out of our good old lady, all the evils she inherits, all the evils she acquires. About the causes of her aches and her pains don't you bother; the 'why' of the obstruction in her bowels of mercy is not of consequence to us. Besides, to be meddlesome is ill-bred. Our concern is to catch the effects; we are intelligent, we shun knowlege of causes. These recipes are sure cure, regardless of the location of society's disease, be it situate anywhere, in any part of the body, from the tip of her great toe to her superior fontanel. They are up and doing, get right on to the difficulty; all that these prescriptions require is to have the disease acute, actively working in the carcass of our good old dame, society. Ladies and gentlemen, could we but catch the original flea that bit the human race, I wouldn't be here this morning at quackery; but we can't; trying is no use, neither can we arrest the biting procession. Guided by the 'legal merits of the case,' society travels on her uppers, has no soul.

"Ladies and gentlemen, I can recommend my first recipe; it has been tried and failed, its virtues therefore are known: increased feudalism. The employer is to love the employé as he does his own son. Going to Chicago, mister? Want the quickest route? 'Jump over the moon.' Surprised at my way of doing, aren't you? That's queer. I'll explain. Either as a tool or head officer, middleman or proprietor, I served the plutocratic cause nigh on to twenty year. Pah! vibratoriness has been known to bring on dizziness, a lasting vertigo; so it is more than likely from the vender's usual way I may be swayed, and to make my doings fit I calculate you will be forced to exercise your own imagination.

"Once upon a time, good folks, the problem was how, dwelling in the midst of moral miasma, to withstand its malarial tendency. The solution has been found. Have little society-scavengers,— mosquitoes, flies; their remedial bites act upon the social whole as a moral quinia. The recipe which I hold in my hand was loaned me by the Ethical Culture Society. Its compounder is lecturing on ethics, how to become moral; is at present stationed in England. My! but that's an unfortunate country.

"You are anxious to test this prescription's virtues? Well, have at it. To give the children food and clothes, to make the family wheels run smooth, without noise, one thing alone is needed, this: let the employer hold back a portion of the workingman's weekly wages and give that portion to the laborer's wife. See stars?

The American version of the Bible says that for idle words one shall be held to strict account; guess that's why our able instructor skipped and went to London. The desert of Sahara might have been a better place to think in.

"Theosophical Society; what a ticket! I've looked into that. Humph! The 'theosofts' claim that a nucleus of universal brotherhood floats in their nebula. Don't you believe it. Why, that nucleus is dead, hasn't a spark of vitality. Their nucleus, however, is the smallest part of the society's property; a monopoly is theirs, a corner in mahatmas. Seen their signboard? 'Inquire within.' To judge from the character of the 'chela's' writings, a mathematical primer, I should say, would be a most useful present to their Koot-Hoomi. Some of their doings have been grotesque enough; of occult forgery a leader was accused; fixed for an investigation was the time and place. To London from America, from India, flocked the officially faithful, but after all the quasi-judicial affair flattened out into a mere burlesque. The lawyer-leader was too cute for minds bent on discovering the unapparent, not by the use of true methods, but through the *ipse dixit* of authority. The plaintiff in this "strange case" through occultism was worsted, and this is how her defeat was brought about. The chela-defendant occupied a double position in that society, vice-president and something else, which I at present do not remember. To find a verdict against Mr. Hyde would naught avail, when in the twinkling of an eye before his peers stood Dr. Jekyll.

"Ladies and gentlemen, I now hold in my hand a recipe, labelled mammoth nonsense. To cure without the aid of surgery society's gangrenous foot, educate the poor, teach them to be skilful workmen."

(*Voice:* "Skip that chestnut.")

"My friend, I thank you. *This* recipe is tied up with a white ribbon; that augers well; attractive, isn't it? Who wagers that, folded inside, a Christ-like sentiment is hid clear out of sight. The Women's Christain Temperance Union strongly urges upon that virtuous, self-sacrificing class, upon employers, the Christian duty of discharging, of rejecting, any laboring man who gets drunk, who takes a glass. Whew! what are they 'giving us' anyway? Does legal robbery, living by profits, does appropriation of the laborer's gain make of the employing class total abstainers? I say, ladies, 'come off the perch'; stealing the devil's livery to serve the Lord in is, to say the least, a shameful thing; by such means you can't raise pariahs. Permit me to remind you that civilization's disinfecting drug is honest equality.

"Here, ladies and gentlemen, is a recipe with something new in it : go down to the poor and teach them how to make the most of the little entrusted to them by the Lord. Hold on just one minute till I fix things up; between poverty and its cause the missing link must be supplied, the word 'gorilla' must be added. Charity works wonders, and this is its how. From the receiver's side, charity supplies all the poor with all necessaries, makes them sure of comforts; by dependence upon charity the impoverished become wise, philosophic, adepts in the art of adaptation, learn how to become all things to all men, that something may be gained thereby. Charity is a soul-architect, is a designer, makes sycophants. From the giver's side, charity makes the donor feel good; to the sense of justice is a gag, to vanity is a bonus. From the standpoint of classes, charity's real meaning is, 'Here, take this pittance, we give you back a paltry portion of that which under money's mask we have stolen.' For society's ailments charity a cure-all? Ugh! silly fools prate of charity.

"Eureka! at last I've got a real novelty, a new phrase: advice to women. Trying to peek at the curiosity? You don't get the chance; I'm in charge, and this rare intoxicating beverage must be taken 'straight.' Teach mothers their responsibility, urge upon them their duty, their ability to produce a brand of sons who shall be independent of environment, who shall inherit none of the father's idiosyncrasies; do you hear that? To think that women have remained ignorant of their powers, of their possibilities! Why, their ignorance must be wilful, for in the matter of advising, of instructing, that sex, we men are never off picket duty; don't know what it is to take a needed rest; morning, noon, and night we are up and at it; in our sleep, even, we don't relinquish the job. The fact is, I sometimes think that by the sum and substance of our talk a monopoly of the somnambulic state is shown to be ours.

"Don't let your interest flag, ladies and gentlemen; don't think me a bore; remember the greatness of the occasion, remember society must be cured. In the grab-bag only a few prescriptions are left. Here is one that is isopathic: To destroy effects, increase their cause; if the shoe pinches your toes, be sane, and tighten the boot so as to have greater pressure. Unrepresented, under paternal government, without chance of *honest* arbitration, the economically oppressed, hearing the still small voice of human wants and human powers, feel themselves outraged, and throw sticks and stones, burn street cars ; guided by animal instinct, they vindicate their cause as best they can. To cure the effects of tyranny, forcible repression of the wronged, pile up tyranny. We live in a republic. KING MONEY orders out the militia : sticks and stones are not *its* missiles. The militia does not burn street cars. KING MONEY has them trained ; their work is destructive, their aim is true ; God's travelling cars are their targets, and anarchist meets anarchist. Whatever is legal is right ; corollary, the isness of the is must be maintained ; capitalism, Lord Gorilla, must be sustained.

" And now, good patient folks, positively this is the last appearing recipe. Its superscription is *Don't*. It combines the virtue of phlebotomy with those of counter-irritant. My good gentleman, on capitalism's Babylonish peak do you securely stand ? in the industrial whirl to the wheel have you put your shoulder, not as man, but as child? If so, you will relish this 'don't.' Don't teach the laboring class that they have natural rights; the truth makes them turbulent, makes them undesirable citizens of our republic."

The morning is far from being spent, shall we not take advantage of our good doctor's versatility? The audience will be pleased to learn that he has consented to tarry and give us a treat, a recitation.

"Ladies and gentlemen, the medley I propose to give is a combination of business acts and of soliloquy. Recital is *my* part, to discover where the laugh comes in is *yours*. Mr. Nibbles, a grocery man on Avenue A, is seated at his desk. Hi, there, Jim, I say, have you sugared that sand? Well then, put this label on: 'Light grade of New Orleans sugar; PURE.' And mind, when the women come in to buy that sweet commodity, tell them the following story, for women have curiosity, and pry into the reason: tell them that unexpectedly I came upon a chance to purchase a large quantity, and that is why I am selling it out cheap; and don't you forget to say that, after all, I only just manage to clear myself, to save a loss. These are ticklish times for a business man, and the women know it. And, Jim, here's a bonus to their feelings : make this remark, accidentally-like, that Mr. Nibbles is an exceptional man, likes to share a good thing, wants to give his customers a benefit ; eh, Jim, and if this venture turns out as I have planned, I'll do a little profit-sharing with you. In the meantime you are learning business methods ; don't forget *that*. Yes, sah. Exit Jim.

"And now Mr. Nibbles thinks aloud. 'I haven't been years in business without learning some few things. I have discovered that women have small sense of honor; in little things are liars ; and then too they are mean and stingy. Why, to save a dime some of them would talk the arm off you ; why is it ? Can't be because women haven't money. I never leave *my* wife without a quarter. She couldn't get along without money ; the thing is impossible; and don't we know that? Men weren't born yesterday. Children have to be fed and clothed, and if sick, why, there's the drugs; and the girl — servants' wages must be paid. And occasionally I *will* have some little delicacy. I own it; I believe in a man being honest, owning up to the corn. Sometimes I need something appetizing. My wife always has money; I take care of that. And so, whatever may be the cause of a woman's stinginess, it certainly is not the want of money. I'd like to know what is the matter with women anyway; must be that their heads are light, top story unfurnished, eh? By Jove, I have hit it; they run mad after fashions, and that's a sign of vacancy, isn't it? Haven't I heard them rave over a color, call it æsthetic? Bah! the silly things.

"'Yes, that's my name; what can I do for you? Pay this bill? Well, let me see it. Fifty dollars for cutting off my horse's tail? Whew! you've gone up on surgery. Case of demand and supply, want to adjust the market to your pocket; I see through it. To cut off Dobbin's tail I paid only twenty-five dollars. I call this raise unfair; it's taking advantage of a man's necessities; you veterinaries must be getting rich, kept steady at such jobs. The men who own horses have just gone mad on this fashion. But, I say, can't you reduce this bill a little, scale it on the score of casualties? Why, the horse isn't well, and may die yet; the spine, by that operation, has received a shock, and, robbed of nature's means of self-defence, the pesky flies have full swing, torment the poor fellow almost to death, irritate him beyond measure. I'm not a fool; of course I know that a mutilated horse is less valuable than a sound one; don't deny the thing is a piece of tomfoolery; but then, what's a man who wants to be in style, wants with his horse to cut a figure, to do? Might as well be out of the world as out of fashion, is an old and true proverb. Here's your money, just receipt the bill. Good-morning, sir.

"'Could we but catch the original robber of the horse race, the man who first began the brutal business, why, then it could be stopped; but we can't, and so, "guided by the merits of the case," by fashion, there is nothing for us but to go on, and on, and on, forever and forever, cutting off poor horses' tails. Heigh-ho! I'm glad it's over; it's a mean piece of business, but then it is heroic. My wife musn't see this bill; lucky it didn't go to the house. Wasn't she opposed, said 'twas cruel, fiendish. But then she calls eating meat, feeding on the corpses of our coexistent ancestry. Women *do* have queer streaks.

"'I am worried; my bank account is getting low, the money till is about empty. That last bet of mine now, had I only won it. Gracious me, but things are lackadaisical. Why is it we men don't get along better? I am sure we try hard enough to keep from going under, try to keep erect and on our economic feet; and I know for a fact that business is conducted on a grand scale; men have brains. Not an honest thing in the market; adulteration is kept jumping, busy in every direction, and yet, after all, in money matters it is the few who have easy minds. My good mother used to say that nothing went without hands, so somebody's extravagance must be to blame for the difficulties of business men. Wouldn't I like to ferret the folly out, whatever it may be. Guess I'll think a minute.**** Great Scott! I have it : our women chew gum. Let me see : "where was I at ?" I'm frustrated by that discovery, that addition to inductive science. I think I was going to make a remark about women. Yes, that's it. I am disappointed in the women, for, what with their limited capacity and the educational advantages they now possess, they ought to make progress, ought to acquire more knowledge of business methods, ought to be, in short, more businesslike. Men try hard, always *have* tried, to stimulate the women to greatness by encouraging them ; morning, noon, and night, they have rubbed their inferiority in on them. Now, my wife in answer declares that talk is vapory, that a tree is known by its fruits ; protests that she is a realist, demands an exhibition of men's superiority; at the same time she says she begs the favor of a "rest" from their boast. What is a man to do under such circumstances, with only the raw material, the power to become, and no finished product on hand? This is the way I get out of the difficulty: I cling to talk. Oak-like, isn't it? I get mad and insist that she's got our exhibition of superiority. Mary Jane retorts by pointing to what she calls sex-precedent, meaning this: a rejoicing rooster on a refuse heap flaps his wings and crows; a hen laid the egg. Mary Jane to me at times is awfully impertinent.

"'Business is dull this morning, customers don't flock in; that's the fault of the women, they are too saving, try to make a little go a long ways; times with business men would be better if the women were inclined to be extravagant.

"'Well, haven't I had a loud reverie. Can't help it. Man has an active brain, and that is why he is so superior to all the rest of creation. Heigh-ho! I may as well keep at it.

"'Educational opportunities, why are they closed to women? The hand of Providence must certainly be in it, for ministers fight woman's progress inch by inch every step of the way. My wife accounts for the mystery by what she calls an occult reason; says that, unconsciously conscious of their deficient start, men, to lessen the gulf between them and the favored sex, the one which had a better God-impulsion, have cornered educational opportunities. Of late years I am not bothered to help the church, either by my presence or with my money. How I did begrudge that last gift, my haul from a lucky bet! All went to fix up a fine altar and to buy for the church an expensive Bible. Mary Jane says she has shed her milk teeth, and is now working to uplift humanity. My wife is a socialist. I don't often come right out with this; it would hurt my business, would injure me with my political party, and so I keep shady; but now I am alone and have nobody to fear; besides, talking aloud makes an imaginative man fancy he is an orator.

"'I take it she wants the brotherly condition brought about. That's too good, ha! ha! ha! As though there would ever come a time when men wont do each other up if there is a chance. My wife wants the state to adopt the family plan; fool notion; shows a woman's ignorance of a man, the image of his Maker. How can women know about the Lord when they make such mistakes? That rib isn't straight'ened out yet; I reckon it isn't working natural. I would like to have some proof of that Bible story; I must ask the college demonstrator of anatomy if he finds men's ribs uneven, more on one side than the other. I more than half believe that sometime that bony explanation will turn out to be a wrong translation, just a crow rigged up to scare the men folks into subjection. But what am I saying? This way of accounting for it wont do; there is a superlative objection: the women had no hand in getting up the Bible, and when found sick, it is divinity that doctors our Holy Book. Let me think: now, if men were started on the race-track physically imperfect, minus a rib, why, then, of course the women folks would come out physically ahead; I'm willing to stake on that. And yet it is the men who vote. Well, I don't understand, unless the knee-pan, at the beginning, was the site of more intelligence than the rib; unless civilization's selective power led to nice sex discriminations, knew exactly where to strike a deathblow. Acquired deficiencies must be more damaging than those deficiencies with which one starts, than natural imperfections are. Is that reasonable, though? Men are not ashamed of ribbal insufficiency, boast of it; men have made the Bible. I am in a muddle; that comes of following suggestion's lead. Well, I am precious sure of one thing: if physical deformity is natural to men, and civilization hasn't helped us out, we are in a pretty box. Woman's day is at hand, and, by George! the revisers better hustle, jump onto that crooked story, make it straight, make it fit in natural with things that are actual.

"'To remonstrants, my wife suggests that they investigate socialism in a rational spirit ; the very existence of society implies socialism in some form or other, so she says ; and the present form is bad, is destructive to that friendliness which it has taken ages to build up ; she protests that our present socio-economic condition leads to prostitution of the human feeling. She meets one objection by reminding me that I do not eat with all the folks whom I meet in the street cars ; declares that fraternal socialism does not entail loving the uncongenial ; that to respect, to love, the principle of right dealing, equality would, in a way natural to humans, bring that state about. When in the course of her argument she turns and with pathos asks, Why leave the well uncovered, knowing that, though George and Mary may escape, John and Bessie must fall in, must drown ?—when into her socialistic talk she brings the children—I own, through fear for their future, I am more than half convinced. You see, it's about other people's children that we men don't care a darn. So limited, Mary

Jane says, the character of our motive is not different from that of the brute mother who provides, fights for, and loves her own children.

"'Once we came near to quarreling. The morning paper told of motherless children shipped to their father who was laboring in the West; went there to get a job. Not being properly notified of the time of their arrival, the poor children had to hang about that Western station. Well, after they had had twenty-four hours of it, hungry and disappointed, all of them broke down and cried. Jerusalem! the folks flew, took them pies and cakes, fixed them up with warm clothes, and found their father for them. It thrilled me through, and I allow 'twas charitable, 'twas grand; but my wife wouldn't see it, said she was disgusted that in a civilized country the social state permitted children to travel alone, permitted children to be neglected; said the only way to get attention, to get one's natural rights, was to make a big noise.

"'Mrs. Nibbles assures me that fraternal socialism will come anyway, and she asks me if the business men care whether the servant girl gets her letters or not. I have to own up that of course they do not, but that the means which ensures *us* an orderly reception of our letters, ensures poor Gretchen hers. I accuse Mrs. Nibbles of being an anarchist, and she admits it; says she wants to destroy everything that is not natural to our industrial methods, everything that is not natural to us as human beings. She accuses those who inveigh against socialism of absurdity, of shutting their eyes to facts, of not seeing that paternal socialism's irritating control trickles through all social layers; says that to please some employers shop girls must wear black; and then she goes off into a merry laugh over male ideas of a free country. Starting with the capitalists, who are the first controllers, she travels on down, shows that between the grocery-man and the butcher the hour for meals is varied, no two of them consecutively are alike, and then she pins me down by asking, Can fraternal socialism do more than to decide what shall and what shall not be produced, and how much of what is in the market one shall have? Can fraternal socialism do more than to interfere with your personal arrangements, interfere with your private affairs? Annoyances from servants? Well, upon this topic my wife don't talk; she thinks that as a class they are abused, and in their defence I have heard her say that the persons she has found most destitute of the moral sense are *not* in the servant girl ranks.

"'Steam heat? Ah! that is a sore point with me. I have had experience, have felt the double bite, frost and burn. Now, I don't like a business joke played on me. One don't want in his home to experience the extremes of temperature, winter and summer, in a single day. Offices are heated by steam; there the square thing is done; but in dwellings? Can it be that they think that, if women and children are mainly the ones to suffer, it don't matter? Well, anyway I have concluded that obtaining tenants under false pretences ought, like obtaining goods, to be actionable. Mary Jane, when I broach the subject, takes in her flag, insists that of course landlords want to turn an honest penny; that it is unreasonable to expect them to make tenants a present of heat. She says that when the sun is shining in Florida, or in the southeast apartment, if the occupants of the northeast flat expect comfort, warmth, they are anarchists. She says that beggars shouldn't be choosers, and avers that one ought to be more than satisfied, having both certainty and surprises combined in a steam-heated apartment, the certainty of uncertainty, and the joyful surprise when warm air *does* come radiating up. But I don't like it; it don't suit me to be frozen one hour and roasted the next, and so I have decided upon a set of questions to be categorically put to landlords and their tools (beg pardon, agents) the next time I rent a steam-heated apartment. This lack of balance in the management of steam heat my wife accounts for by the fact of its male control, the engineer thinking that to give the regulation amount, the quantity KING MONEY'S perquisite allows, is all that is necessary; no cause to growl about the time or the evenness of its coming up.

"'For the people's awful comfort, the principle of inequality, the economic gospel is responsible, Mary Jane says, and I believe that she is about right. Not that I always approve of my wife's views, and I don't often encourage her socialistic talk; it would not do. She is altogether too intellectual, takes after her mother's side of the house. Why, for generations the women of her family have a record of being smart. Now, I know what I am talking about, have investigated this matter, know that Mary Jane has a powerful brain, thinks too much, and that is why I act as moderator. I am a pretty liberal man; my wife says so. That reminds me: I have a friend who says he never believes anything a woman says about her husband, that is, if it happens to be good; says it's natural for a wife to want to make folks believe that her hubby is just too good and smart, and that she will try to do it every time unless she's dead beat out by the man. It is a fact that women are fabricators even over trifles, seems somehow to be their nature, seems to be in grain. But then that's not *my* wife, what *she* says can be depended upon every time ; the higher mathematics ain't more truthful ; and my wife says I am a pretty liberal man. Still, I wouldn't like to see our women in public affairs ; they are too possessed with the idea of uniformity, would congeal things, would obstruct progress. Now, were school affairs under the management of the women, schools in this great city, New York, would for all the children be provided ; thousands of little folks on education bent would not be turned away on the plea of no room inside, be bidden to go roam the streets. That's the way it is now. I am compelled to own that the Political Fathers' method of preparing children to become respectable citizens is disgraceful to an enlightened republic, but the principal of inequality would be denied were every child given schooling opportunity ; it would be imprisoned, confined to its lawful quarters, and then things would be congealed. Medical authority claims that civilization has made changes in woman's knee-pan, unfitted her to vote. Physical deficiency interferes with woman's use of the ballot, but leaves the mentally bow-legged free to exercise the franchise. By Jupiter! I allow that's queer.' Ladies and gentlemen, I bid you good morning."

I am sure that I voice the feelings of this audience when I say that we are grateful to society's quack doctor, and to his double, the reciter, for the lively entertainment they have furnished us this morning; but, Herr Doctor, may I be allowed to make one correction? I think that you called society a dame; now, to that I take exception. Rectify that error in the future; kindly bear in mind that, though unmanly, political society is every inch a man.

Friends, let us suppose that one of us falls ill, sends for a doctor, the case by her is diagnosticated pneumonia. Is she pessimistic? Which of us, if sane, holds that physician responsible for the suffering and the pain, our imminent danger? Ladies and gentlemen, I have great pleasure in introducing the Socialist, who, though last, is by no means the least.

SOCIALIST: "You have sat long, you must

be weary ; I shall endeavor to be brief. Upon society's actual exhibition I shall lightly touch, but upon what society, by implication, *is*, were there time, I would say much. Humor a lover's fancy ; I would personify society as my other self, my better half. I love my wife and I would have her womanly, would have her well.

" Ladies and gentlemen, need I remind you that not an individual thing stands by itself alone ? Relations exist and can be found. Thus the unknowable is reached, and thus all things are unified. Particulars into generals must fit. Humor a lover's fancy ; come with me upon abstract conception's track. Let us imagine a something having vitality, a something that is plastic ; true, carbon, nitrogen, and oxygen, as commonly positioned, are not its elements. The constituents of social-protoplasm are Principles and Powers, the Unknowable on its subjective side. Sifted, you are aware that everything is motion ; in perpetual manifestation are the Principles and Powers, actors in the omnipotence-drama. This granted, you will allow that, given

Om's impulsion, my wife's motion must be ever onward ; unto perfection she approaches through lesser forms ; by and by she will be human, and eventually reach the divine. From resistance to the UP and the ON comes the wayward motion ; into the plans of God such hath not entered ; my Lord Evolution drives Om's stately van. Tossed to and fro are the surface waters, but look into the river's deep, look below ; *there* the current ever onward moves to the ocean, to the sublime.

"By analogy may we not interpret the meaning of the destiny of social-protoplasm, may we not gather lessons from the result of motions by life's physical basis? I think so. Traveling through beings-space, ere protoplasm reached the human form, the detours were many that it made ; collected, boiled down, separated from the froth and the scum, what is the substance of their deep purport? Why, this : a body with a backbone, a head, and a perfectly formed heart,

"Now, wherefore a backbone? Why, to preserve equality in opportunity, and, by preservation of equal natural rights, to co-ordinate the different individual parts into a living organism, into a unified whole, the palace car of OM. Upon the spine a blow, traumatic injury, and, lo! there arises a nervous disorder, disclosed by the uncertain, the wabbling gait. Upon the social spine falls the blow of the Lord Gorilla. Society's walk is reeling; she is not drunken, is diseased; society has locomotor-ataxia.

"Ladies and gentlemen, you know our claims, our socialistic prophecy. Society must become human. Why? Because in social-protoplasm there is the active woman element, the principle of sympathy; it is persistent, and it *will* be expressed *intelligently*. How will this be brought about? and how account for the character of the mode of this coming introduction? Good friends, I leave with you this double conundrum; put head and heart to work, and it is readily seen through.

"Briefly I call attention to some facts which show us by exemplification what we have a right to expect. Church supremacy, in the minds of the people as a whole, has received its death-blow; a twin fetich, divine right of kings, keeps the supreme corpse company. Merely as social institutions the church and monarchy are struggling now to maintain position. The divine right of money holds the fort of supremacy; its feet are getting cold; socialism is at work, the death gurgle comes in time, and then hark: the king is dead, long live King Humanity.

"First, the horde, for subsistence, all did the same thing; new-born humanity was unacquainted with its powers. Differentiation came, and into the clan were introduced the political thought and bad social adjustment. Chattel slavery, long a prevalent mode of service, has gone; in the game of social euchre must wage slavery not follow suit? By the relation of divided parts, by the facts of division and of form — But kindly look upon this demonstration; it will save time and show the sure prophecy of social adjustment's final state, Fraternity, to those at least who sense the meaning of progressive motion:

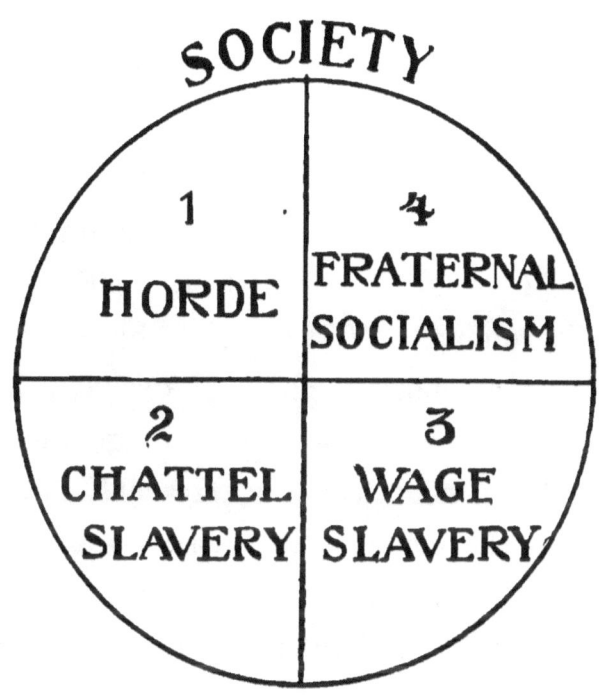

"With the spoils system gone, and Fraternity at home, conduct has no economic chance to be less than human, less than straight and square.

"Will the audience kindly tarry for a moment? I hear a voice; from spirit-land a form is coming. Wearied with the hardships of his lot a laboring child of twelve, a little factory boy down East, lost courage with us to live, but believing in a Heavenly Father he found the courage to depart — suicide by drowning. Hush-sh-sh! he speaks:

"'I wanted to be like other boys, go to school and have playtime, but from morning until night with me was work or starve. I wasn't strong, my legs ached; at last there came a happy thought — run away; but then where to? I didn't know anyone that would take me in, be kind and let me play, and I didn't know what to do, which way to turn, until I thought of heaven and God. It was noon, the sun was shining bright, and seemed to say, "Come right up here, little boy; there's lots of room." I felt encouraged, took my way down to the river's brink; guess a kind spirit helped me, though, and gave me strength. Splash! *** When I woke up an angel had me in her arms. Spirits knew that I was tired. Things up here are good and lovely, and oh! I am so happy and so glad. Good-bye.'"

(The audience is gone and I am anxious to inquire if my wife, for her effort to do good, to sow socialistic seed, feels repaid; am anxious to express the hope that she is happy.)

To give perceptive power is the work of deity; but *our* duty is to help each other unto opportunities to unfold. The soil, I know, was good, and I do indeed feel sure that socialistic seed has taken root. Oh! would that I possessed the magic power to, on the instant, call it up a blossoming tree, another instant, change the blossoms into the perfect fruit.

(Remember all things come to those who wait ; I would my wife were a more patient person. Well, business presses, and I for my engagements am already late. Good-morning ; I shall be home at six.)

"All things come to those who wait." Kindly meant, but by just such phrases folks are gagged; without some one's effort and some one's work, *nothing* comes. Of comforts and luxuries I am possessed, and if I, when thinking upon the wants, upon the galling poverty, of others, feel as I do, what must their sensation be, upon whom the tiger has fixed his tooth and claw? And then to know that it is needless; " aye, there's the rub"; to know that it is because rights and opportunities are pillaged.

No sentiment in business, I have heard it said. Egregious blunder! In sentiment, the sentiment of self, is business soaked. "The struggle for existence" is a phrase that fitted the living fact before productive power grew tall enough to look into the eyes to read the soul of man's environment. The struggle for existence means now class carnage. Were my children crying for bread and I none to give, were my babes pinched by the cold and I powerless to help, I, their mother, to get square with the social monster would feel an eternity too short; and if within my breast the sleeping lion by sympathy is aroused, what wonder if actual sufferers turn demons? I know that, in the future, folks shall live as humans, and by the thought my soul is buoyed up.

The grand social change, how, oh! how shall it be brought about, be ushered in? Shall it be by intelligence directly applied to that end? My house of hope rests not on rock of sand. My expectation on desire's high sea in principles and in REACTION'S power is anchored. Pour into a full vessel and it overflows, clothes are soiled, and the unwise get wet. The fulness of oppression's cup is rising to the brim. Wisdom sought not Adam; could not reach his intellect but through his love of self, through appetite. Wisdom in the guise of serpent went unto the woman.

In my conclusions have I erred? Be charitable, my brothers; excuse, I pray you, on the ground of woman's faulty logic.

The greatest good to the greatest number? Political gag, dead and gone. The greatest good to each, the greatest good to all, mother thought, radiating, alive; fraternal socialism, our socio-economic state centered on the family plan. Nobody pulled down, everybody lifted up, and that social class who from the mathematic point of view morally are robbers, reclaimed, and by sanitary social conditions cured of their disposition to do violent deeds. Excelsior! Not in the possession of happiness, but in the method of its gainment, at the expense of others, selfishness lies. Do not unto others that which ye would not they should do unto you. "Give me a fulcrum, and I will lift the world," says Archimedes. Here brother, take it: *You and me.*

Through the operation of NATURAL attraction, associations formed; in the socio-economic millennium, commingling of the congenial, friendships, every human feeling not trampled upon by KING MONEY.

Did I hear the question asked, What under fraternal socialism must be done with our guardian angels, keepers of reformatory homes for moral monsters, indigent, forlorn, our helpless girls and boys, children for whom Christ did not live and agonize?* * * * *   No, I will not second the motion to send those keepers to * * * *. Why, I have friends there; besides, the invalids in that winter resort ought at least to have a chance to * * * * *   And since my medical opinion has been asked, I prescribe for these protectors of the spiritual, these evolvers of the good, these hatchers of the moral self, the heavenliest, purest atmosphere. A milder form of bliss I think might work a full effect upon their ministerial defenders.

Fraternal socialism, by the law of opposites, in one of two ways must come. By philosophic anarchism shall its advent be? Well, that depends. The earthquake's roar was sudden, likewise the earthquake's appearance, but for a long time the forces had been gathering. The earth's crust was inelastic, would not yield. Examine forts, fill them with ammunition, store your bombs; intimidation is your game. Get ready for an uprising of the people. Tools of KING MONEY slaughter the unrepresented; this is a republic. With the blood of victims natural rights must be bought; this is a republic. With money, with powder and with shot, privileges are purchased. Guided by "the merits of the case" anarchists sustain Lord Gorilla's cause in this republic.

Think to prevent fraternal socialism? Can the accoucheur prevent the birth? Economic methods contain within themselves the "sacred fire." "What can be avoided whose end is purposed by the mighty gods?" Down with vicious legislation. Christians of the millennium, be not afraid; opportunity to fight will still continue; look within, subjugate that monster. Peace, peace; the world wants peace. But the industrial massacre goes on. And the cry goes up, and the cry goes up; shall it never come down? What say the facts of motion? Yea, verily! Plutocrats, be aware! The ball which decends to earth with great momentum received its force from an impelling hand. RE-ACTION is EQUAL to ACTION and in the contrary direction. Is society a band of robber-ruffians, bound together by the bond of mutual murder? Come, let us be human.

And Jesus said, I come nqt to bring peace [TO SINFUL CONDITIONS], but a sword.

THE END.

From the press of the Arena Publishing Company.

A Stirring Drama of War-Times.

Mary Holland Lee

Price, paper, 50 cents; cloth, $1.25.

MARGARET SALISBURY.

The setting of the story is vivid and picturesque, bridging the period of our Civil war, and its touches upon New England and Virginia life are full of local color, provincial phraseology and dramatic power. The tale opens with a description of Three Oaks, a fine Virginia estate, the fate of whose owners is curiously interwoven with the three gigantic trees from which the place receives its name. Mrs. Lee strikes the note of heredity firmly, and the most tragic complication of her plot hinges upon the unlawful use of hypnotic power. The world of books is far too poor in well-told stories of our war, to accord anything less than enthusiastic welcome to this latest comer, so full of rich detail and striking scenes both North and South, and so winning in the even, impartial temper with which the sad struggles of the great Rebellion are incidentally set forth. It will attract that great army of readers which turns to books for amusement and distraction.

"Margaret Salisbury" is the brave and loyal heroine of a stirring drama of the Civil War. Her love story is a sad one and long in telling, but it affords the author opportunity to introduce pictures of Southern life in anti-bellum days and some startling episodes of army times. The sympathetic interest of the reader will be aroused by a succession of unusual incidents. — *Public Opinion*, Washington, D. C.

North and South, their people and principles, are the text of the book. The slavery question is treated from an unprejudiced standpoint. The Negro, Yankee and Southern characters are lifelike under skilful moulding. As a love story it is pure, simple, strong and pathetic. — *The American Newsman*, New York City.

"Margaret Salisbury" is a story of the war, and is charmingly told. Its heroes are of the real kind who believe what they profess because they were born to believe so. The story is enlivened by a vein of rather exquisite humor and toned up by clean, pure and healthy sentiment, altogether furnishing a most entertaining tale of heroic times. — *Kansas City Journal*.

For sale by all newsdealers, or sent postpaid by
    Arena Publishing Co., Boston, Mass.

A Bundle of New Books.

A New Book of Social Thought. JUST PUBLISHED.

Price, paper, 25 *cents; cloth,* $1.00.

B. O. Flower

The Social Factors at Work in the Ascent of Man

The New Time: A Plea for the Union of the Moral Forces for Practical Progress.

This new work, by the author of "Civilization's Inferno," deals with practical methods for the reform of specific social evils. The writer does not bind together a mere bundle of social speculations, that would seem to many to have only a remote and abstract relevance to everyday life. He deals with facts within every one's knowledge. "The New Time" brings its matter directly home to every man's bosom and business — following Bacon's prescription.

It is published especially to meet the wants of those who wish to apply themselves to and interest their friends in the various branches of educational and social effort comprised in the platform of the National Union for Practical Progress; but, from its wide sweep of all the factors in the social problem, it will also serve to introduce many readers to a general consideration of the newer social thinking.

Price, paper, 50 *cents; cloth,* $1.00.

Rev. Minot J. Savage

A New World, a New God, a New Humanity

The New Religious Thinking deals only with Verities

The Irrepressible Conflict between Two World=Theories.

Five lectures dealing with Christianity and evolutionary thought, to which is added "The Inevitable Surrender of Orthodoxy." By the famous Unitarian divine, advanced thinker and author of "Psychics: Facts and Theories." Mr. Savage stands in the van of the progress of moral, humane and rational ideas of human society and religion, which must be inextricably commingled in the new thinking, and a stronger word for moral and intellectual freedom has never been written than "The Irrepressible Conflict." We are now going through the greatest revolution of thought the world has ever seen. It means nothing less than a new universe, a new God, a new man, a new destiny.

For sale by all newsdealers or sent postpaid by
Arena Publishing Co., Boston, Mass.

From the press of the Arena Publishing Company.

Fiction: Social, Economic and Reformative.

Price, paper, 50 cents; cloth, $1.25.

E. Stillman Doubleday

JUST PLAIN FOLKS.

A novel for the industrial millions, illustrating two stupendous facts: —

1. The bounty and goodness of nature.
2. The misery resulting from unjust social conditions which enable the acquirer of wealth to degenerate in luxury and idleness, and the wealth producer to slave himself to death, haunted by an ever-present fear of starvation when not actually driven to vice or begging. It is an exceedingly interesting book, simply and affectingly told, while there is a vast deal of the philosophy of communism in the moralizing of Old Bat. All persons interested in wholesome fiction, and who also desire to understand the conditions of honest industry and society-made vice, should read this admirable story.

A story of the Struggles of Honest Industry under Present Day Conditions.

Price, paper, 50 cents; cloth, $1.25.

Charles S. Daniel

AI : A Social Vision.

One of the most ingenious, unique and thought-provoking stories of the present generation. It is a social vision, and in many respects the most noteworthy of the many remarkable dreams called forth by the general unrest and intellectual activity of the present generation. But unlike most social dreams appearing since the famous "Utopia" of Sir Thomas More, this book has distinctive qualities which will commend it to many readers who take, as yet, little interest in the vital social problems of the hour. A quiet humor pervades the whole volume which is most delightful.

A Story of the Transformation of the Slums

The brotherhood of man and various sociological and philanthropic ideas, such as the establishment of a college settlement and the social regeneration of Old Philadelphia, are a few of the topics discussed in "Ai," a novel by Charles Daniel, who calls it "A Social Vision." It is alternately grave and gay; and the intellectual freshness reminds one constantly of Edward Everett Hale's stories, with which "Ai" has much in common. This is a clever book, and, what is much more important, one whose influence is for good. — *Public Ledger.*

From the press of the Arena Publishing Company.

A Sequel to "Looking Backward."

Price, cloth, $1.25; paper, 50 cents.

Rabbi Solomon Schindler

YOUNG WEST.

The author of "Looking Backward" and others did a good work in introducing to the general reader many ideas which had been discussed for a long time by the best scientific writers of our day, but which were and are unfortunately removed from popular sympathy through the strictly scientific character of the literary vehicles in which they appeared. But the author of "Looking Backward," probably on account of the limited compass of his book, has not given in detail a description of all the social conditions of the brighter future which is to witness the triumph of altruism. He has merely whetted the appetite of the reader, but he has not satified his hunger. "Young West" (the son of Julian West) will indirectly answer all these questions. Describing his own eventful career from his first awakening to consciousness to his age of three-score and ten, the hero of the book will picture life in its various phases, as it will be acted out by a citizen of the United States of America in the twenty-second century.

Civilization under Nationalism in the Twenty-Second Century

The book is intended primarily to answer the many questions which are asked about the practical workings of nationalism and socialism.

A Stirring Story of the War.

Price, cloth, $1.25; paper, 50 cents.

Helen H. Gardener

AN UNOFFICIAL PATRIOT.

This is a story of the Civil War, but it is the first story of its kind that has appeared in our literature. It deals with a phase of the war entirely new in fiction. It is a departure from all Helen Gardener's previous stories, and is perhaps the strongest piece of work she has produced. The *Boston Home Journal* says: "Is in many ways the most remarkable historical novel of the Civil War which has yet appeared. The story is filled with strong dramatic incidents, and there is a bit of charming romance. Mrs. Gardener has produced a book that will take very high rank in the historical literature of the War of the Rebellion; for although presented in the form of a novel, its historical value cannot be questioned."

For sale by all newsdealers, or sent postpaid by
Arena Publishing Co., Boston, Mass.

www.ingramcontent.com/pod-product-compliance
Lightning Source LLC
Chambersburg PA
CBHW032043230426
43672CB00009B/1456